Small World *Big Flavors*

Small World *Big Flavors*

Our Family Legacy

By John and Teresa Polk

Inspired by our family travels, cultures, and generations of love for good food

ISBN Number: 978-0-692-97860-3

Library of Congress Control Number: 2017917188

Publisher: Teresa Polk
11831 338th Ave NE
Carnation, WA 98014

We wish to dedicate this book to our children.

You're fun to travel with in part because you are adventuresome in trying new foods. You inspire us to try doing new things in life.

Contents

Index of Dishes

Appetizers and Snacks

Antipasto Platter
French Onion Dip
Celery with Blue Cheese
Pimento Cheese Spread
Stuffed Mushrooms
Hot Crab and Artichoke Dip
Smoked Salmon Cucumber Appetizer
Ahi Poke with Fried Wontons
Homemade Microwave Popcorn

Soups

French Onion Soup
Beef/ Pork/ Chicken Stock
Roasted Tomato Basil Soup
Cream of Veggie Soup
Curry Squash Soup
Clam Chowder
Shrimp Bisque
Chicken Tortilla Soup
Albondigas (Mexican Meatball Soup)
Hot and Sour soup
Wonton Soup
Egg Drop Soup
Minestrone Soup
West African Peanut Soup

Salads

Seafood Louie
Beets, Goat Cheese and Chicken Salad

Salads- continued

Traditional Coleslaw
Broccoli Salad
Potato Salad
Chef Salad
Niçoise Salad
Caesar Salad
Pickled Beets
German Potato Salad
Taco Salad
Japanese Cucumber Salad
Teriyaki Restaurant Style Salad
Asian Coleslaw
Traditional Greek Salad (Horiatiki)
Italian Antipasto Salad
Italian Pasta Salad
Dijon Italian Dressing
Traditional Italian Dressing
Chunky Blue Cheese Dressing

Main Dishes
Meat and Poultry

Beef Stroganoff
Beef Hungarian Goulash
Piroshki
Meatloaf
Chili for Chili dogs
Cincinnati Chili
Beef Stew- BBQ Style
Reuben Sandwiches

Index of Dishes- Continued

Main Dishes
Meat and Poultry- Continued

Grilled BBQ Beef Ribs
Pork Chops- Brined and Grilled
BBQ Pulled Pork
Hearty Chicken Herb Pot Pie
Grilled BBQ Chicken or Pork Ribs
Spicy Buffalo Chicken Wings- Oven Baked
Buffalo Chicken Wraps
Grilled Lemon Pepper Chicken
Orange Fennel Chicken
Paprika Chicken
Crispy Herb Roasted Chicken
Oven BBQ chicken
Duck Breasts with Plum Sauce
Grilled Chicken Under a Brick
Brined Roasted Stuffed Turkey

Seafood

Jambalaya
Gumbo
Crab cakes
Bacon- Wrapped Scallops or Prawns
Shrimp Scampi
Fried Shrimp
Salmon- Oven Roasted or Pan Fried
Steamed Clams
Spaghetti with Clams

Mexican

Carne Asada
Enchiladas
Tamales
Quesadilas
Carnitas
Mexican Pork
Fried Burritos
Chile Rellenos
Taco Pie
Chili Verde
Red Beef Chili
Tacos
Margaritas

Asian

Kung Pao Chicken
Mongolian Beef Stir Fry
Stir Fry with Rice Noodles
Simple Stir Fry
Grilled Teriyaki Chicken/Pork/Beef
Singapore Chili Crab or Shrimp
Thai Sweet & Sour Pork or Chicken
Thai Sweet & Sour Fish
Korean BBQ Kalbi Beef Ribs

Greek

Grilled Lamb Chops
Lamb Dolmathes

Index of Dishes- Continued

Index of Dishes- Continued

Introduction

Both of us grew up in the fifties through seventies on the foods that were readily available at the time in rural America. It was only later in life after exposure to different cultures and their foods that we became aware of the incredible array of tastes that the world had to offer. My introduction to some of the variety of tastes started for me while attending college in southern California. Then after my junior year in college I took a year off of school and traveled around the world that whole year. At that point it cemented for me so many different foods and flavors to pick from, and the desire to create these dishes at home.

Men making bread in Herat Afghanistan in 1978.

Over the years I've learned to love making foods from scratch, and I've learned just how easy some of it can be; items such as sauerkraut, mustard, ricotta cheese, and blue cheese dressing to name a few. These things can be made so easily, they are a fraction of the cost of what you buy in the store, and they are made from just fresh and healthy ingredients.

I enjoy growing some of my own produce. I routinely plant tomatoes, cukes, and peppers. I also grow many herbs that can really add to the taste of some of the dishes. But nobody has a garden like Teresa's Mom- she grows so many types of veggies, fruits, and herbs, and she has always shared with us. This has enabled us to try veggies we might not have otherwise ventured into, such as Hubbard squash, chard, mustard greens, and tomatillos (and others).

Introduction- continued

We live in Washington where in the summer months and into the fall we go to the Yakima area to get fresh produce in bulk, such as various kinds of peppers and tomatoes for making sauces and freezing. We are often also in Tucson, Arizona for part of the year where we are able to get super fresh produce in the winter months.

From our family to yours- we hope you enjoy our recipes.

John

I wanted to create this cookbook as a legacy for our children. We have a lot of family and friends that enjoy cooking, so we'd like to share with them as well. Over the years we've had many gatherings at our house revolving around delicious meals and wonderful family and friends.

When I was around 11 or 12, my Mom learned to cook Mexican food from a friend and neighbor who also taught her about shopping for various ingredients that are were not at that time available in the typical grocery store. From then on I just loved Mexican food. My mom loved trying new things- I'm sure I got the desire for exploring new foods from her.

Introduction- continued

Then when John and I got married in 1981, we began traveling around in a lot of places in the world. We became exposed to many other cuisines, and we began to learn how to make some of the dishes we had experienced. Today the world is a smaller place and the variety of stores and restaurants, and exposure to the cultures of the world allows us to sample the great food available to us.

John has done most of the cooking at our house. I do cook as well, but nobody can get an absolutely delicious meal on the table after work for the family as quickly as John! If they waited for me to get dinner together after work, they risked dying of starvation....

Both of our kids used to call John up at work and ask "Dad how do I make...?" whatever dish they were dreaming of. They even continued calling him after they left home.

Here's a sticky note that Tim used to make notes while he was on the phone with Dad on how to make meatballs in terminology that Tim could relate with.

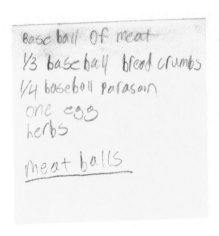

Both of our kids learned the basics of cooking from being involved and helping. And I'm proud to say that as adults now, they have an interest in many different cuisines and they have become great cooks themselves.

Happy cooking (and eating!),

Teresa

Introduction- continued

"it doesn't seem likely a skinny woman can write a cook book that anyone would read..." Jean Hughes Polk 1973

About the artwork and photos

John's mom, Jean Hughes Polk, was a Fine Arts major in college. In 1973 she created the beginnings of a cookbook for her sister, Aunt Georgie. These drawings were sketches that she made for that book. The photos were all taken by us over the course of our travels, gatherings, and cooking.

Notes on Recipes

This book does not address safe handling and sanitation methods that should be used when dealing with eggs and meats, nor the methods for safe freezing and canning. Under-cooking eggs and meats of all types can lead to illness, especially those with high risk factors. Be sure to follow the governmental guidelines for cleaning, separating, cooking, and chilling. The recipes shown in this book illustrate how we make them, each reader must decide on their desired level of doneness.

Our ovens do vary and altitude can make a difference in how the recipes turn out. Everyone knows their own kitchen, so adjust how you use these recipes to accommodate.

Using good ingredients are essential for the recipes to be the best they can be. Examples are what type of blue cheese you use for Blue Cheese Dressing, and homemade stock versus store bought, etc. When we feel it is really important we say in the recipe.

Trust your judgment in deciding ingredient quantities- Eggs come in various sizes, chicken breasts can be enormous or small. Use what you've got on hand and adjust as needed.

If using fresh herbs, use 3 times the amount as called for of dried herbs.

Stir frying is a personal thing, some people prefer veggies cooked more and some less. Some like the veggie pieces larger and some like them smaller. The recipes and methods of cooking reflect using bigger pieces and cooked very lightly. If you prefer veggies cut smaller, the cooking time will be a little less to get the same level of doneness.

Everybody's tastes are different when it comes to the amount of salt and pepper, and when it comes to the level of spice. We tend to use less salt and more herbs and spices in our cooking. We also like a fair amount of spiciness. Do adjust seasonings to your liking.

When a recipe calls for flour to thicken a dish or flour for dredging meats, mochiko (rice flour) can be used instead to make the dish gluten-free. It will generally take a little more mochiko than flour to achieve the same thickness.

We invite you to vary from the recipes to suit your own tastes, styles, and dietary needs.

Appetizers and Snacks

Antipasto Platter

Antipasto means *before the meal*. But we sometimes like it as a main course. This also makes for a fun picnic lunch, since a lot of the items can be finger foods.

Every time we make this it's different- it's fun to use your imagination and come up with a combination of ingredients that go well together and are beautiful to look at, not to mention delicious!

You can size the platter and the number of ingredients you use to the number of people you're serving.

Ingredients ideas:

Meats- choose 2 or 3 cured Italian meat slices such as: Genoa salami, soppressata, prosciutto, or Calabrese

Cheeses- choose 2 or 3 cheeses such as: Fontina, Gorgonzola, feta, Parmesan, small mozzarella balls, or provolone.

Olives- we like to get olives from the olive bar at our local grocery stores. We use any of the black, green, or even stuffed ones. Kalamata go nicely as well.

Veggies- add a couple of things to add to the color and texture of your platter: pickled asparagus, artichoke hearts, pickled pepperoncinis, roasted red peppers, cherry tomatoes, and caperberries.

Directions:

Arrange what ingredients you decide on onto a platter. Your platter can be made ahead and refrigerated until serving time.

French Onion Dip

Makes about 1 1/2 cups

Ingredients:

1/2 large yellow onion, diced
1/2 cup sour cream
1/2 cup mayonnaise (we like Hellmann's or Best foods)
1/4 teaspoon garlic powder
1/4 teaspoon freshly ground pepper
small pinch of salt (or to taste)
extra virgin olive oil for sautéing
chips for dipping

Directions:

Sauté onions in olive oil until soft and caramelized to light brown only. Stir frequently to make sure they don't burn. Once done, let them cool and add to a medium sized bowl. Add the remaining ingredients and stir well. Refrigerate for several hours before serving. This dip is even better the next day. (It doesn't last that long in our house!)

Celery with Blue Cheese

Ingredients:

celery ribs, cut into 2 inch lengths
Chunky Blue Cheese Dressing (see recipe)
extra blue cheese if desired
roasted sunflower seeds
1/4 fresh red pepper

Directions:

Wash and wipe the celery dry. Cut into lengths. Mix the blue cheese dressing with additional blue cheese if it has a runny consistency. Fill the celery with the chunky dressing. Sprinkle sunflower seeds over them. Slice red pepper into super thin slices to be used as garnish.

Refrigerate then serve.

Pimento Cheese Spread

This makes a great make-ahead appetizer. Serve with your favorite crackers and/or celery sticks.

Typically we can only get red bell peppers in the grocery store, but sometimes we can get fresh pimento peppers from Yakima, Washington, and we roast, peel, and seed them, and freeze them for future use- such as Pimento Cheese Spread!

Makes 1 to 1 1/2 cups

Ingredients:

- 1 large roasted red pepper
- 1/2 package of cream cheese (4 ounces) – room temp
- 1/2 cup mayonnaise
- 1/4 teaspoon fresh ground pepper
- 1/2 to 1 teaspoon Tabasco sauce (to taste)
- 8 ounces good cheddar cheese- finely grated

Directions:

Prepare pepper:
Cut pepper in half lengthwise and remove seeds, stem, and ribs. Place the pepper on a sheet pan, skin side up, and broil until the skin is blackened almost all over.   Be careful not to cook the peppers too much (they can get mushy). Put the roasted pepper in a plastic bag with about a teaspoon of water and tie the bag, trapping air in it to let the pepper steam until cool. Remove the skin that comes easily off. Don't worry about any skin still on and do not rinse, this adds flavor. When cool enough to handle, chop and set aside. You can also roast the peppers the day before and let steam and cool in the fridge and keep them in the fridge overnight. This makes the peeling even easier.

Prepare cheese mixture:
In a mixing bowl, stir together the cream cheese, mayo, Tabasco, and black pepper until fully mixed and smooth.   Add in the grated cheddar. Once all mixed, add the red peppers and stir. Refrigerate before serving.

Stuffed Mushrooms

Stuffed mushrooms can be made with any number of ingredients- it depends on what you are in the mood for and what you have on hand. You can use cooked sausage and then top with cheese, or you can use just chopped veggies as in this recipe and put bread crumbs on top. Instead of Parmesan, you can use a different cheese such as blue cheese or Fontina. Serves 4 as an appetizer or side dish

Ingredients:

12 medium or 8 large cremini mushrooms
3 tablespoons extra virgin olive oil
1/2 cup finely chopped yellow onion
2-3 cloves garlic, finely chopped

1/4 cup bread crumbs
dash of hot pepper sauce
3 tablespoons Parmesan cheese, grated
3 tablespoons finely chopped fresh parsley

Directions:

Clean the mushrooms and then remove the mushroom stems and chop. If desired, you can add extra chopped mushroom as well. Heat a saucepan to medium. Add oil and then onions, mushrooms, and garlic, and cook until soft. Remove from heat and add 2 tablespoons bread crumbs, parsley, hot pepper sauce, and cheese. Mix until well combined. If the mixture looks too dry, add more olive oil. Season the mixture with salt and pepper to taste. Fill the mushroom caps with the mixture.

Sprinkle some bread crumbs on top of each mushroom. Drizzle olive oil over the tops of each mushroom.

Bake mushrooms in a 350 degree (F) oven for 20 minutes or until mushrooms look cooked through. If making them to time with other dishes, cook only 15 minutes then turn oven off and let them sit until ready to serve.

Hot Crab and Artichoke Dip

Appetizer for 4

Ingredients:

3/4 cup mayonnaise
2 tablespoons juice from lemon
1 cup artichoke hearts, chopped
   (fresh cooked or canned)
1 cup cooked, shelled crab meat
1/2 cup grated Parmesan cheese
3/4 cup grated jack cheese
bread or chips for serving

Directions:

In a medium bowl combine the mayonnaise, lemon juice, Parmesan cheese, and jack cheese, reserving some of the jack cheese for the top. Mix until incorporated. Add the crab and artichokes, and mix gently. Grease a small oven proof dish with olive oil. Add crab and artichoke mix to the dish, and sprinkle remaining jack cheese over the top.

Bake at 325 degrees (F) for about 20-25 minutes until it's bubbling and starting to brown.

Serve while hot with French bread croutons, pita chips, or tortilla chips.

Smoked Salmon Cucumber Appetizer

This is a delicious and healthy make-ahead appetizer that we just love!

Serves 4

Ingredients:

    1 English cucumber cut diagonally in slices
    1/2 package cream cheese
    1 slice of fresh lemon (optional)
    smoked salmon (can use either smoked or lox)
    dill for garnish

Directions:

Prepare the lemon by slicing the lemon very thin (about 1/16 of an inch thick). Cut the lemon slice into very small pieces.

Cut cucumber slices, and place on a platter. Use a paper towel to remove any excess water from them. Carefully dab on about 1/2 teaspoon of cream cheese onto each cuke piece. Place a small piece of smoked salmon on top the cream cheese. Place a lemon piece on the salmon. Sprinkle dill over the platter to garnish.

Ahi Poke with Fried Wontons

In Hawaii, every family has their own ahi poke recipe (pronounced poh-keh), and it's served at many family barbeques and nearly every restaurant. While we are not Hawaiian, we have family members that are. It's not only ono (delicious) it's fresh and healthy too! Serves 4

Ingredients:

1 pound sushi-grade raw Ahi tuna-
    diced 1/2 inch across the grain
1/4 cup sweet onion – julienne cut
3 tablespoons green onions thinly sliced
4-5 tablespoons soy sauce

1-2 teaspoons toasted sesame seeds
very thin slices of serrano pepper (optional)
1/4 teaspoon kosher salt or to taste
1/2 teaspoon toasted sesame oil
1 lime- cut into wedges for garnish

Wontons:

wonton wrappers
oil for frying (peanut or avocado)

Directions:

Whisk together all ingredients except for tuna. Combine dressing with the raw tuna and refrigerate for 2 hours. Serve with fried wonton wrappers and lime wedges. Lime squeezed over the top when serving really adds!

For the wontons: Cut wontons into wedges or strips for dipping. Deep fry and transfer to paper towels to drain. Season them with salt and serve immediately.

Other options are to add finely chopped macadamia nuts. Instead of using sliced chili pepper, you could use rooster sauce or sambal sauce. Some people like to add fresh grated ginger.

Traditional Hawaiian Poke includes Ahi Tuna, chopped macadamia or cashews, roasted seaweed, Hawaiian sea salt, and some sliced chili peppers.

Homemade Microwave Popcorn

This is way healthier than and just as easy as the premixed microwave packages!

Ingredients:

1/4 cup popcorn kernels
1 tablespoon olive oil
1/4 teaspoon salt
paper lunch bag (new)

Flavorings of your choice:

melted butter
garlic powder
Parmesan cheese
macadamia oil
anything else you can think of

Directions:

Mix together popcorn kernels, olive oil, and salt in a bowl. Place paper bag on an oven and microwave-safe plate. Put popcorn mix into paper bag. Fold the bag edges twice to prevent it from opening in the microwave. Cook in the microwave for up to 3 minutes, stopping the microwave when there is 1-2 seconds between pops. Carefully open the bag (it's hot!), and pour popcorn into a serving bowl. Add your favorite flavoring to the popcorn and stir. Enjoy!

Soups

French Onion Soup

Making your own stock for this soup really adds. Serves 3-4

Ingredients:

1 quart Beef Stock (see recipe)
   -or- 1 quart store bought stock plus 2
   teaspoons dried thyme
3 large onions cut in half, then sliced
extra virgin olive oil

2 tablespoons butter
Gruyère or Swiss cheese slices
French or other sturdy bread cut into slices
additional 1 teaspoon of thyme
salt and pepper to taste

Directions:

Sauté the onions in olive oil and butter until the onions are very soft and starting to brown. Add stock to the onions, add additional thyme, and heat through. Taste and add salt and pepper as needed.

The classic way to melt the cheese is to float a slice of bread with a cheese slice on top of an oven-proof bowl and put it under the broiler. We prefer to broil the bread slices with cheese slices on top by themselves and then float them in the soup when we are ready to serve.

Beef/ Pork/ Chicken Stock

You can buy the stock but this makes soup so good!

Ingredients:

4 pounds beef bones (or less if meaty)
2 carrots washed and cut into 2 inch pieces
1 large onion cut into 8 pieces
1 tomato cut into 8 pieces
1 stalk celery cut into 2 inch pieces
1 large clove garlic rough chopped

5 sprigs fresh parsley
2 teaspoons dried thyme
2 bay leaves
1/2 teaspoon salt
1 teaspoon peppercorns

Directions:

Place beef, onion, and carrots in a large Dutch oven and roast in a 450 degree (F) oven for about 1/2 hour to brown. Add remaining ingredients, cover with water, and then simmer on the stove for 2 1/2 hours, or until the marrow has dissolved. Strain, and skim fat. It's easiest to make this the day before and refrigerate so the fat will solidify on top for easy removal. If making pork stock, use same recipe as for beef.

To make chicken stock there is no need to brown the bones first. Just put the bones in a large pot, add the veggies and water, and cook it as you would with beef broth. Strain it, let cool, and then remove the fat.

Note: We like to save the trimmings from various types of onions, carrots, and celery as we use them, and put them in the freezer in a large zip bag for use for this stock. There's no need to process them in any way- just keep adding raw veggie trimmings to the zip bag that's in the freezer until ready to use. Be sure to wash the outsides and get rid of any end that may still have dirt on it before adding to the bag. It's surprising that the onion paper, carrot peelings, celery stalk center and leaves can add so much flavor! If using the frozen veggie trimmings instead of whole veggies, do not roast with the beef. Just add them to the pot when you add the water, and you'll be straining the veggies out of the broth when it's done. Since this tastes so good, we're all in favor of reducing the waste.

Roasted Tomato Basil Soup

Serves 4

Ingredients:

2 pounds ripe Roma tomatoes or other plums

1/4 cup plus 2 tablespoons good olive oil

1/2 teaspoon kosher salt

1 teaspoon freshly ground black pepper

1 cup chopped yellow onions

1 celery rib, cut into large pieces

celery leaves from several ribs, chopped

1/2 medium carrot diced

2-3 garlic cloves, minced

2 tablespoons butter

1/8 teaspoon red pepper flakes (to taste)

1 28-ounce can San Marzano tomatoes & juice

1/4 cup fresh basil leaves, chopped

1 1/2 teaspoon dried thyme

3/4 teaspoon dried oregano

2 cups chicken stock or broth

chopped basil for garnish

croutons (see directions below)

Directions:

Cut tomatoes in half lengthwise, and remove seeds and any hard core pieces. Toss the tomatoes with 1/4 cup olive oil. Spread in 1 layer on a baking sheet skin side up, and broil for about 10 minutes, or until most of them have charring on the skin. Allow the tomatoes to cool enough to handle. Remove any skins that are not charred and discard. Keep the skins on the ones that are charred- this add a lot of flavor.

In a large pot over medium heat, sauté the onions, celery, carrots, and garlic with 2 tablespoons of olive oil, the butter, and red pepper flakes, until the onions start to brown. Add the canned tomatoes, herbs, chicken stock, and basil. Chop the roasted tomatoes, and add to the pot, including the liquid on the baking sheet. Bring to a boil and simmer covered for 30 minutes. Remove cover and simmer 10 minutes more. Remove the large celery pieces and discard. Use a blender or stick blender to make smooth. Taste for seasonings, and add salt if needed at this point. Simmer 10 minutes more uncovered. Pour to bowls, garnish with fresh chopped basil and croutons, and serve while hot.

Make croutons ahead by using left-over French bread or artisan bread. Cut into 1/2" cubes, and place in a plastic bag. Pour olive oil into the bag, and shake to coat. Toss in just a pinch of salt (optional) and other desired seasonings, such as thyme, parsley, and/or oregano. Shake again to coat. Pour coated bread out onto a cookie sheet, and bake at 350 degrees (F) until crisp, about 12-15 minutes. No need to flip them while cooking.

Cream of Veggie Soup

We just love cream of asparagus or cream of broccoli soup, but you could use this recipe for any number of vegetables, such as cauliflower, mushrooms, and more.

Serves 4

Ingredients:

1/2 yellow onion, chopped
2 tablespoons flour
4 cups chicken stock or broth
1 1/2 pound vegetables
3/4 cup half and half
salt and pepper
4 tablespoons butter
pinch of cayenne pepper (optional)

Directions:

Sauté onions in 2 tablespoons butter until soft. At the same time, also add the firm stems from broccoli or cauliflower pieces if using. Whisk in the 2 tablespoons flour. Add the chicken broth and the remaining vegetables, and simmer until vegetables and onions are tender. A pinch of cayenne pepper with the chicken broth adds a bright flavor.

Remove a few pieces of veggies to add back in later. Puree the rest using a stick blender, blender or food processor. Add in the half and half, and heat just until the soup thickens, don't bring to a boil. Add salt and pepper to taste, and finish with 2 tablespoons more of butter. Add the reserved veggies and serve.

Curry Squash Soup

Teresa's mom grows Hubbard squash, and sometimes has one she cannot use. She typically grows them and processes enough to have in her freezer to last to the next year. In 2016 she gave us one so big we could hardly carry it home! We cut it into manageable sized pieces and then baked the pieces at 350 degrees (F) covered with foil (no water in the pan) until soft. Depending on the size, it will cook from 45 minutes to 1 1/2 hours. We then froze the cooked squash in portion sizes. This makes for quick, easy and yummy side dishes. You could also use acorn or butternut squash for this recipe. Serves 2

Ingredients:

2 cups cooked squash	1/2 teaspoon ground cumin
extra virgin olive oil	1 tablespoon grated fresh ginger
2 tablespoons butter	2 cups chicken stock or broth
2/3 cup yellow onion, chopped	salt and freshly ground pepper to taste
2 teaspoons regular curry powder	sour cream for garnish
pinch of cayenne to make spicy (optional)	chopped fresh cilantro for garnish
1/4 cup half and half	

Directions:

Sauté onions in olive oil until they are soft, and add the butter. Once melted, add the spices and grated ginger. Sauté about 1 minute, then add the squash and chicken broth.

Simmer until the squash is fully cooked and heated through. Use a stick blender to make smooth. Continue simmering until thickened to your liking. Add salt and pepper to taste.

Add in the half and half, and heat just until the soup thickens, don't bring to a boil. It's ready to serve! Serve, and garnish with sour cream and cilantro.

Clam Chowder

This is not a thick and 'flour-y' chowder, but it is full of flavor and delicious! The paprika and cayenne make it have a slight reddish color unlike the traditional white chowder.   Serves 4

Ingredients:

51-ounce can clams with juice
5 slices bacon
3 tablespoons butter
1/2 large onion chopped
1 rib celery finely chopped
5 tablespoons flour

2 medium potatoes cubed (we like Yukon Gold or fingerlings)
2 1/2 cups half and half
2 teaspoons paprika
1/4 teaspoon cayenne (optional)
salt and freshly ground pepper

Directions:

In a large pot, sauté bacon until crisp, and drain leaving the fat in the pan. Set bacon aside for garnish. Add the butter to the pan, and sauté the vegetables until soft. Add 2 tablespoons flour and incorporate well. Add the juice from clams and potatoes. Simmer until potatoes are tender.

Mix the remaining 3 tablespoons of the flour in with the half and half, and strain to remove lumps. Add the half and half, paprika, and cayenne to the pot, and heat just until the soup thickens, don't bring to a boil. Taste, and then add salt and pepper as desired. If using salted butter, adding salt may not be necessary since the clams also have salt. Serve in bowls, and garnish with crispy bacon pieces.

Shrimp Bisque

Serves 4

Ingredients:

   1 pound large wild raw shrimp
   4 cups shrimp stock (see recipe below)
   2-4 tablespoons olive oil
   2 leeks- chopped white and light green parts
   2 ribs of celery, chopped, including some
       extra leaves from the stalk
   2 cloves garlic- chopped
   4 tablespoons butter
   4 tablespoons flour
   2 cups half-and-half
   3 tablespoons tomato paste
   1/2 teaspoon kosher salt or to taste
   1 teaspoon freshly ground black pepper
    pinch cayenne pepper

Directions:

Peel and de-vein the shrimp, and reserve the shells. Place the shrimp shells and 5 cups of water in a saucepan, and simmer for 15 minutes only. Strain and set stock aside.

Meanwhile, heat the olive oil in a large pot. Add the leeks and celery, and cook them on medium-low heat, until the leeks are tender but not browned. Add the garlic, and cook 1 more minute. Add the cayenne pepper and shrimp, and cook over medium to low heat for 3 minutes stirring occasionally. Make sure shrimp are cooked through. Transfer the shrimp and leeks mixture plus one cup of the stock to a blender, and process until pureed to desired level. You may want to leave a couple of cooked shrimp whole for adding to the bisque while serving.

In the same pot, melt the butter. Add the flour, and cook over medium-low heat for 1 minute stirring with a spatula to make a roux. Add the remaining shrimp stock, and cook for about 3 minutes, stirring, until thickened. Stir in the pureed shrimp, tomato paste, salt, and pepper, and bring back to a boil. Add half and half, and heat just until the soup thickens, don't bring to a boil. Check seasonings, and add salt and pepper, or cayenne as desired. Serve to bowls, and garnish with remaining cooked shrimp.

Chicken Tortilla Soup

Serves 4

Ingredients:

1 large chicken breast
6 cups chicken stock or broth
1/2 tablespoon garlic, finely chopped
1/2 large onion, chopped
2 tablespoons chopped cilantro
1 15-ounce can of diced tomatoes
1 teaspoon cumin
1 tablespoon ancho chili powder

1/4 tablespoon dried oregano
2 bay leaves
salt and freshly ground pepper to taste
1 poblano pepper
juice of 1/2 lime
kernels off of 1 ear of fresh corn
1/4 cup masa mixed with 1/2 cup water
1/2 jalapeño pepper, seeded and finely chopped

Garnish:

1/2 jalapeño, seeded and sliced very thinly
chopped cilantro leaves
corn tortilla chips or strips (see below)
diced avocado
grated Monterey Jack cheese

Directions:

Roast the poblano: Cut pepper in half lengthwise and remove seeds and stem. Place the pepper on a sheet pan, skin side up, and broil until the skin is blackened almost all over. Put the roasted pepper in a plastic bag with about a teaspoon of water and tie the bag, trapping air in it to let the pepper steam until cool. Remove the skin that comes easily off. Don't worry about any skin still on and do not rinse, this adds flavor. When cool enough to handle, chop and set aside.

Cook the chicken: Cut the breasts to half thickness, add to a small pan, and cover with water. Bring chicken and water to a boil, and let boil only 30 seconds to 1 minute, and turn the heat off. Let chicken and water sit for 3 minutes, and then remove chicken to a bowl. Once cool enough to handle, shred the chicken. Spoon ¼ cup of the hot cooking liquid into the chicken, toss, and set aside. As the chicken cools, it will absorb most of the liquid.

In a large pot, sauté onions, garlic, and chopped jalapeño in olive oil until soft. Add chicken broth, tomatoes, poblanos, lime, cilantro, and spices. Simmer for about 1 1/2 hours. In the last 20 minutes, add the corn. Also add the masa mixture to thicken the soup to the desired thickness. When the soup is done cooking, add the chicken, and bring back to a boil. Check for seasonings, and add salt and pepper if needed. It's ready to serve with all the garnishes!

Tortilla strips:

Lightly paint 3-4 tortillas with olive oil, and cut into strips. Sprinkle a little salt, and bake on a sheet pan at 350 degrees (F) until brown, no need to turn them.

Albondigas (Mexican Meatball Soup)

Using your homemade beef stock makes this soup delicious! You can also substitute some of the beef stock with chicken stock. Serves 4-5

Ingredients:

1 pound lean ground beef
1/4 cup masa
2 eggs
6 cups Beef Stock (see recipe)
1 tablespoon dried oregano
1 large onion, chopped
2 medium carrots, sliced

1/4 to 1/2 cup rice
2 teaspoons chili powder
1/3 cup fresh cilantro leaves, rough chopped
some cilantro leaves for garnish
lime, cut into wedges for garnish
salt and pepper to taste

Directions:

Mix together the beef, masa, and eggs. Form into 1 1/2 inch meatballs, and set aside.

In a large uncovered pot, combine the rest of the broth, oregano, chili powder, and chopped onions, and bring to a boil. Add the meatballs. Bring back to a boil, and then add the rice and carrots. Cook uncovered until the rice and carrots are done, about 20-25 minutes. By this time the meat should be cooked through. Alternately, the rice can be cooked separately, and then added to bowls when pouring the soup. This allows for whether or not to include rice as a low-carb option.

Taste, and add salt and pepper as needed. Add the 1/3 cup of chopped cilantro leaves. Stir, and remove from heat. Serve in bowls garnished with cilantro leaves and a lime wedge.

Hot and Sour Soup

Serves 2-3

Ingredients:

1 small chicken breast
1/2 cup mushrooms (we like Shimeji or Enoki)
4 cups chicken stock or broth
1/4 teaspoon fresh ground black pepper
3 tablespoons soy sauce
1/2 cup rice vinegar
2/3 cup bamboo shoots, julienned

3 ounces firm tofu, cut into 1/2-inch cubes
1 1/2 tablespoon Garlic Chili Sauce
2 tablespoons corn starch
1 egg, beaten
2 chopped green onions
1/2 teaspoon sesame oil

Directions:

Precook the chicken breast: Cut the breasts to half thickness, add to a small pan, and cover with water. Bring chicken and water to a boil, and let boil only 30 seconds to 1 minute, and then turn the heat off. Let the chicken and water sit for 3 minutes, and then remove chicken to a bowl. Once cool enough to handle, shred the chicken. Spoon 1/4 cup of the hot cooking liquid into the chicken, toss, and set aside. As the chicken cools, it will absorb most of the liquid.

In a large saucepan, bring the 4 cups of chicken broth to a simmer. Add the soy sauce, chicken, mushrooms, vinegar, and garlic chili sauce. Simmer about 5 minutes. Then add the pepper, bamboo shoots, and tofu. Simmer about 5 minutes more.

In a glass or jar, add a little water to the cornstarch, and add this mixture to the soup. Let simmer until thickened, about 3 or so minutes. Stir the soup, and stream the beaten egg in while continuing to stir.

Turn off the heat, and stir in the sesame oil. The green onions can be added at this point, or served as a garnish in the bowls.

Wonton Soup

Serves 4

Ingredients:

Wontons:

- 1/2 pound ground pork
- 24 wonton wrappers
- 2 green onions, diced
- 1 teaspoon soy sauce
- 1/2 teaspoon sesame oil
- 1 tablespoon freshly grated ginger
- 1 tablespoon Shaoxing rice wine

Soup:

- 6 cups chicken stock or broth
- 1 teaspoon soy sauce
- 2 green onions, cut into large pieces
- 1/2 to 3/4 inch ginger, cut into slices
- salt to taste
- 2 green onions chopped for garnish

Make the wontons:

Mix pork, chopped green onions, soy, sesame oil, grated ginger, and Shaoxing wine. Dust your work surface with flour. Put about a 1/2 to 3/4 tablespoon of filling in the wonton. Paint the edges of the wonton with a little water, then fold the wonton diagonally (tip to tip). Seal the edges together with your hands. Curl the tips around and pinch them together, using a little water to moisten them. They should look something like tortellini. Put finished wontons on a plate, and keep them covered with plastic wrap as you work to prevent them from drying out. They can be made ahead if covered and refrigerated.

Make the soup:

Using a large sauce pan, add broth, soy, large green onion pieces, and ginger slices. Boil for about 15-20 minutes to let the flavors blend. Remove large onion and ginger pieces. Taste for salt and add as needed. Leave green onion and ginger in for stronger taste, and remove when the soup cools. Broth can also be made ahead.

When ready to eat, bring broth back to a boil, and add the wontons. Cook about 5-7 minutes until the wontons are translucent. Remove from heat, and serve into bowls. Sprinkle chopped green onions into each bowl.

Egg Drop Soup

Serves 4

Ingredients:

6 cups chicken stock or broth
4 1/8-inch slices of fresh ginger
1 tablespoon soy sauce
2 eggs
2 green onions
1 tablespoon cornstarch or arrowroot powder
salt and freshly ground pepper to taste

Directions:

Peel ginger, and cut slices about 1/8 inch thick. Use the flat side of the knife to smash the ginger pieces a little to release the oils. Break the eggs into a small jar with a lid, and shake until beaten a bit. Set aside.

Chop the green onion, and separate the white and green parts. Set aside. Dissolve the cornstarch or arrowroot powder in a little water. Set aside.

In a medium saucepan, bring the broth, soy sauce, and ginger to a boil. Simmer for 10 minutes. Remove the ginger pieces and discard. Add the white onion pieces. Taste and add salt and pepper as desired.

Bring back to a boil, and stir the soup to get it swirling. Slowly drizzle the beaten egg into the soup while stirring. Add the cornstarch or arrowroot, and bring to a boil to thicken. Once it has thickened, remove from heat, and add the green onion pieces. You're ready to serve!

Minestrone Soup

Serves 4

Ingredients:

2 leeks, white parts chopped
extra-virgin olive oil
2 28-ounce cans tomatoes, including juice
4 cups of beef broth or stock
6 strips bacon- cooked, chopped
1 14-ounce can kidney beans, drained (optional)
3-4 medium size carrots, cut in pieces
1/4 to 1/2 pound green beans, cut in pieces
4 tablespoons fresh oregano, or 4 teaspoons dried
3 teaspoons dried thyme
salt to taste
1 teaspoon freshly ground pepper
1/4 to 1/2 teaspoon red pepper flakes (optional)
1 cup macaroni or shells (optional)
flour to thicken (optional)
Parmesan cheese for garnish (or Romano)

Directions:

In a large pot, cook the chopped bacon until fairly brown and rendered. Remove the bacon, and leave the fat. Add a little olive oil if needed, and sauté the leeks until soft. Add the tomatoes, broth, and herbs. If using whole tomatoes, chop them before adding. Add the kidney beans (if using), bacon, a pinch of salt, and the pepper. Cook covered for about 1 hour to blend the flavors. Taste and add salt if needed. Mix about 3-5 tablespoons flour with about ½ cup water to be used as a thickener, if desired. Add the green beans, carrots, and flour mixture, and cook covered for about 45 minutes. Add macaroni the last 20 minutes. If the soup still needs to thicken, cook uncovered last 20 minutes.

Serve with grated Parmesan cheese on top, and a nice baguette. Mmmm. This hearty soup is good as a side dish or as the main event.

West African Peanut Soup

Serves 4

Ingredients:

1 1/2 chicken breast- uncooked, diced
6 cups chicken broth or stock
1/2 large onion, diced
1 tablespoon garlic, minced
1 tablespoon fresh ginger, minced
1 tablespoon sesame oil
2 1/2 teaspoons curry powder (mild, hot or mix)

3/4 teaspoon crushed red pepper
3/4 teaspoon freshly ground pepper
3/4 teaspoon salt
2 tablespoons tomato paste
1 14-ounce can diced tomatoes
1 cup chunky peanut butter
peanuts for garnish- roughly chopped

Directions:

Sauté onions, garlic, and ginger in the sesame oil until very soft. Add the curry powder, red pepper flakes, salt, and pepper. Add the broth, tomato paste, canned tomatoes, and diced chicken. Bring to a boil, and simmer until the chicken is cooked through, about 10 minutes.

Remove from heat, and stir in peanut butter until fully incorporated. Taste and add salt or pepper, or additional peanut butter as needed. Ready to serve!

Salads

Seafood Louie

Serves 4

Ingredients:

1 1/2 pounds fresh Dungeness crab
    and/or shrimp
asparagus, about 4-5 per person
lettuce- torn to pieces
1 large tomato cut into wedges
-or- cherry tomatoes

1/2 cucumber, sliced
4 hard- boiled eggs, cut into wedges
1 or 2 ripe avocados, sliced
black olives- about 4 per person
lemon wedges- 1 wedge per person

Simple Louie Dressing:

1 1/2 cups mayonnaise
    (Best Foods or Hellmann's)
1/4 cup ketchup
1 1/2 tablespoon sweet pickle relish
1 teaspoon lemon juice
freshly ground pepper to taste

Directions:

This is a great make-ahead kind of meal.
Cook ahead and cool the asparagus, hard
boiled eggs, and crab and/or shrimp, and shell
the crab and shrimp. (The asparagus should
be only lightly cooked). Make the dressing,
and store it in the fridge. When it's time to
make the meal, it's a simple job of cutting
veggies, and assembling the salads. Serve
with the dressing on the side- let each person
add their own.

Other ideas: fresh cooked beets go great in
this salad. Cook ahead, cool, and cut into
wedges. You will never find this in a
restaurant Louie, but if you are beet lovers like
us, try it!

Beets and Goat Cheese Salad with Chicken

Serves 4

Ingredients:

2 medium sized beets
2 whole chicken breasts
goat cheese crumbled
-or- can use feta or blue cheese
1 head green leaf lettuce

1 cup dried cranberries
2 tomatoes cut into wedges, or cherry tomatoes
sweet onion, or red onion, cut into thin slices
1 cup walnuts
raspberry vinaigrette dressing

Directions:

Cook beets well ahead and cool. Cook by washing, then placing them (unpeeled) in a saucepan, and covering them with water. Bring to a boil, and boil them for about 45 minutes or until mostly fork tender. Do not over-cook. Drain them, and refrigerate until well chilled. Peel the skins off, and cut into wedges or slices as desired. They are ready to go on the salad!

Prepare all the salad ingredients and set aside. Prepare the chicken breasts by cutting the two breasts in half horizontally, making each breast into 2 thinner pieces. Pound any areas if needed to gain an even thickness. Season with salt and freshly ground pepper, and cook the chicken your favorite way- pan fry, broil, or grill on the BBQ. Once fully cooked, cut each piece into slices to be put on top the salad.

Prepare individual plates of salad, and top with chicken and vinaigrette dressing.

This is a great summer lunch or dinner, and oh so easy!

Traditional Coleslaw

Ingredients:

cabbage, finely sliced then chopped
green onions, finely chopped
carrots, grated
green peppers, finely chopped

Dressing (makes about 1 cup)

1/2 cup mayonnaise
1/4 cup white wine vinegar
1/4 cup sugar, to taste
1/4 teaspoon celery salt
freshly ground black pepper

Directions:

Mix dressing ingredients together, and set aside. Chop vegetables- enough for the crowd you are serving, and mix together. Drizzle dressing onto salad to the desired amount. This is a great make-ahead dish, as it will sit in the fridge after being dressed for a couple hours with no problem. The left over dressing will keep in the fridge for up to 2 weeks, just shake or stir to reuse.

You could make this super colorful, fun, and delicious by using red and green cabbage, red onion, and/ or red and green peppers.

Broccoli Salad

Serves 4

Ingredients:

Salad:

- 2 heads broccoli cut into bite sized pieces
- 6 slices bacon, cooked and chopped
- 1/4 cup red onion, finely chopped
- 4 ounces cheddar cheese, cut into small cubes
- raisins, or grapes cut in half (optional)
- sunflower seeds- optional

Dressing:

- 3/4 cup mayonnaise
- 2 tablespoons apple cider vinegar
- 2 tablespoons sugar
- 1/8 teaspoon salt
- 1/4 teaspoon freshly ground pepper

Directions:

In a small jar with lid, combine the mayonnaise, vinegar, and sugar. Shake until fully mixed. Refrigerate until ready to use.

Bring a large pot of water to a boil. Add the broccoli pieces, and blanch until bright green and slightly softened, about 2 minutes. Drain and run under cold water to stop the cooking. Drain well, and refrigerate until ready to use.

Meanwhile, cook bacon in oven in single layer on a sheet pan on 350 degrees (F) until crisp; drain on paper towels. Chop bacon into pieces. Let cool, but do not refrigerate.

When ready to serve, stir in the salad ingredients, pour the desired amount of dressing, and toss to coat everything. Serve immediately.

For a low-carb version, you could use Xylitol (sugar alcohol) or another sugar substitute instead of sugar.

Potato Salad

We like a little crunch in our potato salad, so we like to add some chopped veggies. In our family, potato salad is very free form, so you could make it this way one time, and add other ingredients the next time. We've used sliced black olives and/or chopped bacon in the past. What we add depends on what's in the fridge! If we have fresh dill, we sometimes chop that and add it too. Serves 4-5

Ingredients:

4-5 medium to large potatoes
4 eggs, hard boiled and copped
1 or 2 dill pickles, chopped
2 celery ribs, chopped
4-5 green onions, chopped
8-10 radishes, chopped
3/4 cup mayonnaise (Best Foods or Hellmann's)
1/2 cup sour cream
5 teaspoons Dijon mustard
2 teaspoons apple cider vinegar
freshly ground pepper to taste
salt to taste

Directions:

To hard boil the eggs, put them in a pan with water covering them. Bring to a hard boil. Turn the heat down to a low boil and cook for 10 minutes more. Remove from heat and drain. Refrigerate until fully cooled.

Peel the potatoes, and cut into quarters. Place them in a large pot, and cover them with water. Add a pinch of salt. Bring to a hard boil, stirring occasionally to make sure they are not sticking. Turn down to a low boil. Let cook about 15 minutes or until a fork will go thru them, yet they are still firm. Remove from heat and drain. Refrigerate them until fully cooled.

In a small bowl, mix together the mayo, sour cream, vinegar or pickle juice, salt, pepper, and Dijon. Set aside.

Chop the cold potatoes into 1/2 to 3/4 inch pieces. Chop all of the rest of the ingredients, and add to a large mixing bowl. Add the mayonnaise mixture and stir. Put into a serving bowl. If desired, garnish with a sprinkle of paprika, and serve!

Chef Salad

Chef salad is more of an idea than an actual recipe. You can put any of a wide variety of vegetables, as well as meats, cheeses, and eggs. We like to make it because it's a whole meal in itself. Each time we make it, it's different, it just depends on what we have on hand or what we're in the mood for.

Consider using John's Chunky Blue Cheese Dressing or an Italian dressing (see recipes).

Sample Ingredients:

romaine, green leaf or butter lettuce
tomato wedges or cherry tomatoes
carrot, sliced or grated
chopped green onions
cucumbers, sliced or chopped
red pepper, chopped
meat cut into strips- (ham, chicken, turkey or even tuna is great)
cheese cut into strips- (cheddar, Swiss or Provolone works well)
dressing of your choice
hard boiled eggs, cut into quarters
black olives

Niçoise Salad

Ingredients:

Salad:
lettuce (mix of butter lettuce and romaine)
1 1/2 pounds fresh ahi or yellow-fin tuna fillet
1 bunch fresh green beans
2 medium tomatoes, or cherry tomatoes
1 1/2 pounds baby red potatoes or fingerlings
1 small red onion, thinly sliced
4 eggs
Niçoise olives or Kalamata olives
2 tablespoons capers (optional)

Dressing:
1/3 red or white wine vinegar
2/3 cup extra-virgin olive oil
3 tablespoons finely chopped shallot
1 tablespoon chopped fresh thyme
1 tablespoon chopped fresh oregano
1 teaspoon Dijon mustard
salt and freshly ground black pepper

Directions:

If using sushi-grade tuna, you can cook it just seared. If using other fish, you need to fully cook it. Both work awesome for this recipe. Other fishes that work well for this are swordfish and halibut.

Make the dressing by adding the ingredients to a jar with a lid. Shake and set aside.

Add the green beans to boiling water and cook for about 4 minutes, until they are just cooked. Drain and run under cold water to stop them cooking. Hard boil the eggs to medium about 9 minutes.

 Fill a medium size pan with water, and bring to a boil. Add salt to the water. Add the potatoes, and cook until fork tender, 10-25 minutes, depending on size. Drain and let cool. Once cool enough to handle, cut potatoes in halves or quarters, or cut fingerlings lengthwise. Put them in a bowl. Add about 1/4 cup of the dressing to the potatoes while they are still warm. As they cool, they will absorb it. Set potatoes aside.

Lightly season the tuna with salt and pepper, and fry them in a hot skillet until seared on the outside and still pink on the inside. Slice across the grain into 1/4-inch strips. Alternately, you can grill it by brushing the hot grill with oil, and rubbing oil on the tuna.

Assemble salads, including tuna. Shake dressing, and drizzle over salad and serve. You can serve on individual plates or on a large platter and have everyone take the things they like.

Caesar Salad

Dressing:

Salad:

3 medium cloves garlic, pressed or finely grated
1 tablespoon anchovies, finely chopped
1 egg yolk (or 1 tablespoon mayonnaise)
3-4 tablespoons juice from lemon
1/2 cup oil- light olive or avocado
1/4 teaspoon Worcestershire sauce
1/8 teaspoon salt
1/4 teaspoon freshly ground pepper

romaine lettuce- rough chopped
1/2 to 1 cup grated Parmesan cheese
croutons (see below)
Caesar dressing
lemon wedges for garnish

Directions:

Make the garlic and anchovies into a paste. To do this, we use a mortar and pestle, but you could also use the blade of a knife going back and forth over the cutting board crushing the garlic and anchovies to get the paste consistency. Add egg yolk, lemon, salt, pepper, Worcestershire sauce, and the paste to a blender. Blend until mixed well. While blending, stream in the oil slowly until the oil is incorporated and the dressing is emulsified. You could do this in a bowl using a whisk as well. Refrigerate for at least 4 hours to allow the flavors to blend and the garlic to mellow a bit. The dressing will keep refrigerated and covered for a week or more.

Make croutons ahead by using left-over French bread or artisan bread. Cut into 1/2" cubes, and place in a plastic bag. Pour olive oil into the bag and shake to coat. Toss in just a pinch of salt (optional) and other desired seasonings, such as thyme, parsley, and/or oregano. Shake again to coat. Pour coated bread out onto a cookie sheet, and bake at 350 degrees (F) until crisp, about 12-16 minutes depending on their size. No need to flip them while cooking.

When time for dinner, assemble the salad. In a large bowl, combine rough-chopped romaine lettuce, desired amount of the dressing, some Parmesan cheese, and croutons. Toss to coat and serve with lemon wedges.

Pickled Beets

Our family loves beets made several ways- we like them just boiled and not pickled also. We like the non-pickled variety served hot with a little butter, and we like them served cold- maybe with a salad. Teresa's mom gave us beets with the greens on, fresh right out of her garden. Wow! We typically cook the beets and greens separately to make sure the greens are not overcooked. Beet greens are really delicious too!

T's mom and her Mom, Agnes used to add a little less sugar, and then also add cinnamon and cloves. That's always an option too.

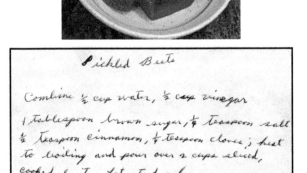

Serves 4

Ingredients:

3 medium beet bottoms
1/2 cup water
1/2 cup apple cider vinegar
2 tablespoons sugar
1/8 teaspoon salt
dash of freshly ground pepper

Directions:

Clean beets, and place in a large sauce pan, and cover with water. Boil them on medium heat, whole and with the skins on. Depending on the size of the beets and how high the heat is, they will take around 45 minutes to 1 hour or more. Cook them until they are fork tender, but still a bit firm. For extra-large beets, it's OK to cut them in half to boil.

Mix the rest of the ingredients together and set aside.

Drain the cooked beets, and let them cool enough to handle. Peel them, cut off the stem ends, and cut them into wedges or slices- however you like them. Put the cooked beets in a bowl, and cover them with the water/ vinegar solution. Refrigerate them for 3 to 4 hours, and then drain off the liquid.

Keep in the fridge until serving time. These will keep in the fridge for up to several days and still remain firm. Delicious!

German Potato Salad

Serves 4-5

Ingredients:

4 large potatoes, such as Yukon Gold
1 teaspoon, plus 1/2 teaspoon kosher salt
3 strips bacon (about 2 ounces), minced
1/2 medium yellow onion, chopped
3/4 cup low-sodium chicken broth

1/3 cup white wine vinegar
1 tablespoon plus 1 teaspoon Dijon mustard
1 teaspoon sugar
freshly ground black pepper
1/4 cup chopped green onions

Directions:

Cut potatoes into quarters. In a large saucepan, place the potatoes in a large saucepan, and add 1 teaspoon of salt. Add water and cover by 1 inch. Bring to a boil, lower the heat, and simmer until just fork tender, about 15-20 minutes depending on size. Drain, transfer to a large bowl, and cover to keep warm.

Meanwhile, heat a small saucepan to medium heat and add the bacon. Cook stirring frequently until crispy. Lower the heat to medium-low. Add the onion and cook, stirring, until translucent, about 6 minutes. Add the remaining 1/2 teaspoon salt, broth, vinegar, mustard, and sugar. Bring to a boil while whisking constantly. Remove from the heat. Cut the potatoes into 1/4 inch slices or 1/2 inch cubes. Return the potatoes to the large bowl. Pour vinegar mixture over the potatoes and very gently toss to coat. Toss in the green onions, and season with pepper to taste. As the potatoes cool, they will absorb the vinegar mixture. Serve while still warm. Toss once more just before serving.

Taco Salad

Taco salad is great as a main dish. But sometimes we have a small salad sans the shell as a side dish to go with other Mexican dishes, such as enchiladas or tamales. Serves 4

Ingredients:

4 large flour tortillas
1 pound ground beef
-or- 2 chicken breasts
Mexi-Mix Seasoning (see recipe)
salt to taste
1 head lettuce, chopped
2 tomatoes, chopped
1/4 sweet onion, chopped
1 cup cheddar cheese, grated
olive oil for tortillas

Sample Garnishes:

sour cream
Salsa (see recipe)
Guacamole (see recipe)
-or- avocado slices
pickled jalapeño slices
cilantro
roasted jalapeños

Directions:

Preheat oven to 350 degrees (F). Paint both sides of the tortillas with oil. To get them to end up bowl shaped, put one inside a large metal bowl or draped on the outside of a smaller metal bowl to bake. Bake for 15 minutes, or just until firm. Remove tortilla from bowl and place directly on oven rack. Bake a few more minutes to desired doneness and crispness. If using only one bowl, bake one tortilla at a time. They are easy to make ahead of time and set aside until ready to make up the Taco Salads.

Cook ground beef until fully cooked in a saucepan. Drain fat, then add desired amount of seasonings. Add about 2 tablespoons of water if needed to make mixture moist. To make shredded chicken, cover chicken breast in a saucepan with water, and cook until fully cooked. Drain, reserving the broth. Shred the chicken and place back in the saucepan with some of the broth. As the chicken cools, it will absorb some broth. Once the broth is absorbed, drain liquid if needed. Add seasonings and mix.

Chop all the veggies. Put the lettuce, tomatoes, onions, and grated cheese in the tortilla shells. Add the meat and garnish with your favorites!

Japanese Cucumber Salad

Serves 4

Ingredients:

2 medium or 1 large cucumbers
1/4 cup rice vinegar
1/4 teaspoon kosher salt (less if using soy sauce)
1 teaspoon soy sauce (optional)
1-2 teaspoons toasted sesame seeds
2 teaspoons sugar

Directions:

For this recipe Kirby or English cucumbers work best, but we use what we've got on hand and it turns out great. Wash and peel stripes from cucumbers. Slice them super thin- 1/8 inch thick or thinner. Put the cucumbers on a paper towel, and using another paper towel, blot the moisture out of them.

In a small dish, mix together the vinegar, salt, soy sauce if using, and sugar until fully dissolved.

When ready to serve, pour what seems to be the right amount of vinegar mixture on the cucumbers, and then sprinkle sesame seeds over the top. They're ready to serve.

Often we can find sesame seeds in the bulk foods section and we just toast our own. It's way less money and super simple. Just put the seeds in a frying pan with nothing else and toast over medium-low heat. You have to watch them and stir them. They are done when they are a very light golden brown. You can also taste them to see if they are done.

Teriyaki Restaurant Style Salad

Dressing Ingredients:

- 1/2 cup mayonnaise
- 1/8 teaspoon garlic powder
- 3 tablespoons rice vinegar
- 2 tablespoons sugar
- 1/2 teaspoon sesame oil
- 1/2 teaspoon soy sauce

Using this kinpira peeler makes the job of julienning the carrots very simple. It is easy to find at an Asian food store or online.

Directions:

Put all dressing ingredients in a pourable glass jar and shake well. Refrigerate for several hours before serving to integrate ingredients.

Teriyaki Restaurant Style Salad is typically only iceberg lettuce with a few julienned carrots. We like to add diced green onions and cucumber as well.

Asian Coleslaw

This is a great side to serve with kalbi beef or teriyaki.

Serves 5-6

Dressing:
- 1/4 cup rice vinegar
- 1/2 tablespoon sesame oil
- 1/2 tablespoon olive oil
- 1 tablespoon soy sauce
- 1/2 tablespoon grated fresh ginger
- 1 tablespoon brown sugar
- 1/8 teaspoon red pepper flakes (optional)

Toss with:
- 1/2-1 head Savoy or Napa cabbage sliced thin and chopped
- 2-3 grated carrots
- 4-5 green onions, sliced thin
- 1/4-1/2 cup cilantro leaves, chopped
- 1/4 cup chopped cashews (optional)

Traditional Greek Salad (Horiatiki)

Salad:

tomato
cucumber
red, orange, and/ or green bell peppers
sweet or red onion, thin slices and quartered
Kalamata olives
feta Cheese
pepperoncini (optional)

Dressing: (for a salad large enough to serve 4)

6 tablespoons extra virgin olive oil
2 tablespoons fresh squeezed lemon juice
1-3 teaspoon red wine vinegar, depending on taste
1/2 teaspoon each oregano, thyme, and ground rosemary or 1 1/2 teaspoon each, fresh chopped
salt and freshly ground pepper to taste

Directions:

Make dressing up to 3 hours ahead, serve at room temperature.

Cut tomato, cucumber, peppers, and pepperoncini into pieces. Add onion slices and olives. Feta can be cut into cubes or crumbled for a family style salad, or simply sliced and placed on top individual salads, which is traditional in Greece.

This recipe has an oil and vinegar type dressing recipe that is more typical in the U.S., but not as much in Greece. They may use only olive oil or maybe also a little lemon, in addition to salt and pepper and herbs.

Italian Antipasto Salad

This makes a great starter course for a crowd. We like to make it on a large serving platter, and people can take which portions of the salad suit them. It's different every time we make it depending on what we have on hand.

Serves 4-6

Sample Ingredients:

romaine and iceberg lettuce mix, chopped/ torn into pieces
large diced or sliced dried salami, prosciutto, soppressata, or any Italian meats
large diced or sliced provolone or mozzarella cheese
pepperoncini, sliced, or served whole
roasted red pepper, large diced or sliced
artichoke hearts, large pieces
cherry tomatoes, cut into halves
red onions sliced thin and cut into quarters
Kalamata Olives
an Italian dressing (see recipes)

Directions:

Arrange on a platter starting with the lettuce and onions. Then add the other ingredients however you wish. Create a pattern, or be random!

Italian Pasta Salad

This is a great make-ahead dish for a crowd.

Ingredients:

cooked and cooled rotini pasta
dry salami, cut into cubes
feta or mozzarella cheese, cut into cubes
cherry tomatoes, cut in halves
Kalamata olives, cut in halves lengthwise
pepperoncini, seeded and sliced
roasted red pepper, sliced
red onion, thin sliced and quartered
an Italian dressing (see recipes)

Directions:

Choose what ingredients suit you for this salad. Other options include artichoke hearts or fresh red peppers instead of roasted. You can use your imagination!

Make pasta ahead and store in a plastic zip bag in the fridge. Slice, chop, and refrigerate all of the ingredients, keeping them each stored separately.

When it's time, just toss all of the ingredients except the feta cheese together and add the dressing. Stir to coat, and then add the feta and stir gently. The feta is delicate; this will help it stay intact.

Italian Dressings

Directions:

Mix all of the ingredients into a pourable container and shake well. Let sit for several hours before serving in order to mix the flavors. Shake before each use. The olive oil will solidify when refrigerating it, but will turn liquid again by just leaving it out on the counter for a few minutes before use.

Dijon Italian Dressing

Ingredients:

1/3 cup apple cider vinegar (or your favorite vinegar)
1/8 cup water
2/3 cup good extra virgin olive oil
1 teaspoon Dijon mustard
1 1/2 teaspoon dried oregano
1 teaspoon dried rosemary, ground
1/2 teaspoon freshly ground pepper
1/4 teaspoon salt

Traditional Italian Dressing

Ingredients: As an option, a teaspoon of Dijon mustard could be added. Instead, you can add a tablespoon of finely grated Parmesan cheese.

1/2 cup extra virgin olive oil
1/4 cup lemon or vinegar or mix of both
3 tablespoons water
1/2 teaspoon oregano
1/2 teaspoon paprika
1/4 teaspoon thyme

1/4 teaspoon garlic powder
1/4 teaspoon onion powder
1/4 teaspoon celery seed
1/4 teaspoon freshly ground pepper (to taste)
1/4 teaspoon salt (to taste)

Chunky Blue Cheese Dressing

John likes to make this dressing using a really strong and delicious blue cheese such as Maytag, Stilton or Point Reyes.   Sometimes we make it very cheesy, sometimes we make it just 'chunky', depends on what we're in the mood for. Either way, it's delicious! Using the best ingredients makes all the difference in this recipe.

Makes about 1 cup.

Ingredients:

1/3 cup mayonnaise (Best Foods or Hellmann's)
1/3 cup sour cream
1 tablespoon lemon
1/8 teaspoon pepper
1/3 cup crumbled blue cheese, or more as desired.
3 tablespoons half and half or cream

Directions:

In a small bowl, add the mayo, sour cream, lemon, and pepper. Add 1/2 of the blue cheese, and using a fork, mash the cheese into the other ingredients. Mix until smooth and cheesy. Add half and half a little at a time until you get the desired consistency. Sprinkle in the remaining cheese crumbles and stir. Add more cheese if even a chunkier consistency is desired. Refrigerate then serve.

Note: As the dressing sits in the refrigerator it will thicken. Before serving check the consistency, and add more half and half, if needed, and stir.

Unused dressing may store in a jar in the refrigerator for up to 1-2 weeks.

Main Dishes

Meat and Poultry

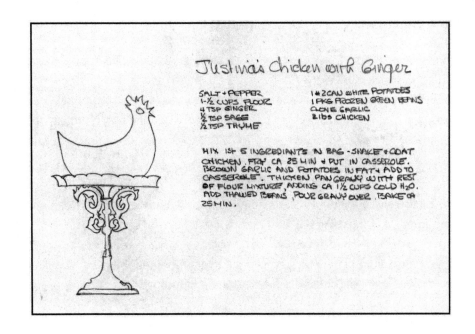

Justinia's Chicken with Ginger

SALT + PEPPER
1-½ CUPS FLOUR
4 TSP GINGER
½ TSP SAGE
½ TSP THYME

1 # 2 CAN WHITE POTATOES
1 PKG FROZEN GREEN BEANS
CLOVE GARLIC
2 lbs CHICKEN

MIX 1st 5 INGREDIANTS IN BAG - SHAKE + COAT
CHICKEN , FRY CA 25 MIN & PUT IN CASSEROLE.
BROWN GARLIC AND POTATOES IN FAT+ ADD TO
CASSEROLE. THICKEN PAN GRAVY WITH REST
OF FLOUR MIXTURE , ADDING CA 1½ CUPS COLD H₂O.
ADD THAWED BEANS , POUR GRAVY OVER , BAKE CA
25 MIN .

Beef Stroganoff

Serves 2

Ingredients:

1 pound filet mignon or sirloin
avocado oil for frying
3 tablespoons butter
1 small onion, sliced
2 cups mushrooms, thick sliced
1/2 cup beef stock or broth
1 tablespoon Dijon mustard

1/4 cup heavy cream or half and half
1/2 cup sour cream
2 teaspoons flour
2 tablespoons minced fresh dill or 2 teaspoons dried
2 tablespoons minced fresh parsley
salt and freshly grounded black pepper
8 ounces medium egg noodles, cooked

Directions:

Cut beef into 2 inches long, 1/4 inch wide strips. Mix broth, mustard, heavy cream, and sour cream together and set aside. If using dried dill, add that to the liquid mixture.

Heat large fry pan on medium-high heat, and add oil. Once hot, add the meat in a single layer, and sear meat on both sides just until cooked, about a minute. Remove to a plate.

Add more oil if needed, add mushrooms to the hot fry pan, and sauté on medium-high heat to get caramelization. Remove to a plate. Add onions to the hot pan, and lower heat to medium. Sauté onions until soft and caramelized.

Add the butter to the pan with the onions and melt. Add the flour and cook while stirring for a minute. Whisk in liquids and any meat juices, and simmer until sauce thickens, about 5 minutes. Return meat and mushrooms to sauce and heat, just until meat is warmed through. Add salt and pepper to taste. Stir in fresh dill and parsley.

Serve with egg noodles.

Hungarian Goulash

Spicy, rich and delicious!

Serves 3-4

Ingredients:

1 1/2 to 2 1/2 pounds beef shank or round
2 tablespoons extra virgin olive oil
2 medium onions, sliced
3 garlic cloves, minced
1 teaspoon caraway seeds, toasted and ground
1 1/2 tablespoons sweet paprika
1 1/2 tablespoons spicy paprika
2 tablespoons fresh chopped marjoram

1 tablespoon chopped fresh thyme
2 bay leaves
1/2 6-ounce can tomato paste
1 14-ounce can chopped tomatoes
2 tablespoons red wine
1 tablespoon balsamic vinegar
4 cups chicken or beef stock
salt and freshly ground pepper
1/2 cup sour cream

Directions:

Cut the beef into 2-inch cubes and set aside. In a large sauté pan, heat the olive oil, and sauté the onions until caramelized. Remove and sear beef. Add the garlic, paprika, and caraway seed, and cook for 2 minutes. Add the marjoram, thyme, bay leaves, canned tomatoes, pepper, vinegar, stock, onions, and the tomato paste. Bring to a boil, then lower to a simmer covered at first and uncovered to thicken during last 1/2 hour until meat is very tender, about 1 1/2 hours, stirring occasionally.

Taste and adjust seasoning with salt and pepper, then add sour cream and serve.

Serve with egg noodles or Spätzle (see recipe).

Piroshki

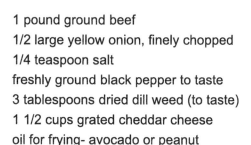

Makes about 12 pastries

Ingredients:

1 (.25 ounce) package active dry yeast
1 cup milk
3 jumbo eggs
1/2 cup oil- avocado or olive
1/4 teaspoon salt
4 cups all-purpose flour

1 pound ground beef
1/2 large yellow onion, finely chopped
1/4 teaspoon salt
freshly ground black pepper to taste
3 tablespoons dried dill weed (to taste)
1 1/2 cups grated cheddar cheese
oil for frying- avocado or peanut

Directions:

Cook the ground beef over medium heat until browned. Drain if needed. Stir in the onion and cook with the beef until translucent. Add salt, pepper, and dill. Let cool, and then mix in the grated cheese. Set aside.   In a small pan over low heat, warm the milk and gently whisk in the eggs, oil, and salt. Remove from heat.

Mix half the flour and the yeast in a large mixing bowl. Gradually stir in the milk mixture. Add the remaining flour a little at a time, stirring after each addition to mix well. Pour out onto a floured work surface. Knead until the dough forms a ball and does not stick to your hands. (Note: More flour may be needed. Add a little at a time as you knead the dough). Place in a well-oiled bowl. Cover the bowl with a clean cloth, and set in a warm location. Allow to rise until doubled in volume.

Place dough on a lightly floured surface. Cut into equal-sized pieces about the size of golf balls. Roll the pieces into disks about 4 inches in diameter. Using a muffin pan, press the disk into a cup. Fill the center of the disk with about 2 tablespoons of the cooled meat and cheese. Fold dough over the meat, and firmly pinch edges to seal. Turn the roll out onto your work surface. Using your hands, roll into a smooth ball, and place on a sheet pan lined with parchment paper. Repeat with all the rolls. Allow to sit and rise for 10 minutes. When letting them sit, cover them with plastic wrap so they don't dry out. At this point, the piroshki can be frozen. Just cover them, and put the sheet pan in the freezer. Once frozen, they can be packaged in individual plastic zip bags. Allow them to thaw before using.

In a small saucepan or skillet with sides, heat oil to 375 degrees (F). Fry the piroshki until golden brown on one side; gently turn and fry the other side. Use a plate with paper towels to drain any excess oil. They are ready to serve.

Meatloaf

Serves 4

Ingredients:

1 1/2 pounds ground beef (grass-fed is good!)
1/2 cup breadcrumbs (or can use oats)
1/2 cup finely chopped yellow onion
1 large egg, lightly beaten
1 tablespoon Worcestershire sauce
1/2 teaspoon of salt
1/2 teaspoon freshly ground pepper
3 tablespoons half and half
1/2 cup ketchup- good quality brand
1 tablespoon olive oil to coat pan

For Roasting: (optional)
2 medium potatoes, cut into quarters
1/2 to 1 large yellow onion, cut into wedges
2 large carrots, peeled and cut into large pieces

Directions:

In a small bowl, lightly beat the egg; add the Worcestershire sauce, half and half, salt, and pepper. Set aside. Use less half and half if using a jumbo egg.

Using a large mixing bowl, add the ground beef, onions, bread crumbs, and egg mixture. Mix together, being careful to not overwork the beef.

Lightly coat a large oven baking pan with olive oil. Using your hands, shape the meat into a 'loaf' shape and pat it so that it stays together while it cooks. Be careful not to squish it together hard, or you will get a dense texture. Place the loaf in the middle of the pan. Place all of the roasting veggies all around the meatloaf to fill the rest of the baking pan. Pour ketchup onto the top of the meatloaf and spread out to cover the top.

Bake at 350 degrees (F) for about 1 to 1 1/4 hours, depending on how wide and tall the loaf is, and depending on the size of the veggies. It's ready when the meatloaf is at 160 degrees (F) inside and the veggies are fork tender. Move meat to a serving platter and let sit for 10 minutes before cutting. Move veggies to a serving dish.

Chili for Chili Dogs

This is great for making Chili Dogs- just grill some good hot dogs, and then top the dogs with chili, and add grated cheddar and chopped sweet onions. Serves lots!

Ingredients:

2 pounds lean ground beef
2 ribs celery + leaves, chopped fine
1 small onion, chopped fine
2 jalapeños seeded and minced
5 cloves garlic minced
cilantro stems, chopped- 1/4 cup
1 28-ounce can tomatoes
1 small can tomato paste

2 cups beef stock or broth
12 ounces beer (such as Guinness)
2 tablespoons cumin
5 tablespoons ancho chili powder
2 teaspoons oregano
pinch salt
extra virgin olive oil for sautéing

Directions:

Sauté celery, onion, jalapeños, cilantro stems, and garlic in a little olive oil until soft. Add the beef and cook until the beef is browned. If using ground beef that is not lean, drain any excess fat off. Add the remaining ingredients, and simmer covered for 3 1/2 hours, stirring occasionally. If it needs to thicken, take the cover off the last 30 minutes.

This could easily be transferred to a crock pot to feed a crowd chili dogs. You could also freeze in portion sizes for chili dogs and chili burgers in your future.

Cincinnati Chili

Our household likes Cincinnati Chili "Four Ways", which is chili, spaghetti, cheese, and onions.   The addition of kidney beans would make this "Five Way" chili.   Serves 3-4

Ingredients:

1 pound extra-lean ground beef	1/2 teaspoon cayenne pepper
1 large onion, chopped	1/2 teaspoon salt
1 clove garlic, minced	1 1/2 tablespoons unsweetened cocoa
1 tablespoon chili powder	-or- 1/2 ounce unsweetened chocolate bar, grated
1 teaspoon ground allspice	1 15-ounce can tomato sauce
1 teaspoon ground cinnamon	1 tablespoon Worcestershire sauce
1 teaspoon ground cumin	1 tablespoon cider vinegar
1/4 teaspoon ground cloves	1/2 cup water or beef stock
grated cheddar cheese for garnish	1 16-ounce package uncooked spaghetti pasta
chopped sweet onion for garnish	

Directions:

In a large sauce pan over medium-high heat, sauté onion, ground beef, garlic, and chili powder until ground beef is slightly cooked.

Add allspice, cinnamon, cumin, cloves, cayenne, salt, cocoa, tomato sauce, Worcestershire sauce, cider vinegar, and water or broth. Reduce heat to low and simmer, covered, 1 hour 30 minutes.   If it looks too watery, you can cook uncovered for part of that time.

Cook spaghetti according to package directions, and transfer onto individual serving plates or bowls. Ladle chili over the spaghetti, and top with grated cheese and chopped sweet onions.

Beef Stew- BBQ Style

Sauce Ingredients:

1/2 cup finely chopped yellow onion

2 cloves garlic, minced

1 cup ketchup

3 tablespoons molasses

1/2 tablespoon brown sugar

1 cup water

1/4 cup cider vinegar

1 tablespoon chili powder

1 tablespoon yellow mustard

1 tablespoon Worcestershire sauce

1/8 teaspoon salt

Rub Ingredients:

1 tablespoon packed brown sugar

1 tablespoon sweet paprika

1 teaspoon garlic powder

1/2 teaspoon dry mustard

1/2 teaspoon ground black pepper

1/4 teaspoon cayenne pepper (optional)

1 teaspoon celery salt

Stew Ingredients:

2 to 3 pounds beef for stew

carrots and potatoes, cut into large pieces

yellow onion, cut into large wedges

any other veggies you like

4 tablespoons flour

Directions:

Mix the rub ingredients together in s small dish. Cut the meat into 2 1/2 to 3 inch cubes. Pat the rub into the meat. Place the meat in a Dutch oven. Mix sauce ingredients in a bowl, and pour over meat. Cook at 325 degrees (F). for 2 hours with the lid on.

Remove meat onto a plate temporarily. In a separate dish, add 2 cups cold water to 4 tablespoons of flour and mix. Add the water/flour mixture to the liquid in the pan.

Turn meat over, and add back to the pan and toss in the carrots, large-cut onions and potatoes. Add more water at this point if needed. Cook with the lid on for 1 hours more. Meat should be tender, and vegetables cooked, but firm. Faster cooking veggies can be added after carrots and potatoes are given a head-start.

Reuben Sandwiches

We like Reubens both with corned beef and with pastrami. You can use any kind of rye bread you like, but we prefer Jewish rye. Reubens are great served with coleslaw or a simple green salad. Serves 4

Ingredients:

2 pieces of rye bread per sandwich
1 1/2 pounds cooked corned beef or pastrami
1 cup sauerkraut (for homemade, see recipe)
Reuben Dressing
Swiss cheese- 1 or 2 slices per sandwich
2-4 tablespoons butter for frying

Reuben Dressing:

1 cup mayonnaise
1/4 cup ketchup
1 1/2 tablespoons sweet pickle relish
1 teaspoon lemon juice
freshly ground pepper to taste

Directions:

Butter 1 side of every slice of bread. Put 1 slice per sandwich, butter side down, into a frying pan. Spread 1-2 tablespoons Reuben dressing on each slice in the pan, followed by about 1/4 cup sauerkraut, sliced meat, and cheese. Spread some more Reuben sauce on top of the cheese. Butter the remaining bread slices and place on top of the sandwiches in the pan, butter side up.

Turn the pan on medium-low heat. Fry the sandwiches until they are golden brown on the first side, about 10 or 15 minutes. Using a spatula, flip the sandwiches onto the second side and fry until golden brown. By this time, the cheese should be melted and the sandwich heated through. Serve while hot.

Grilled BBQ Beef Ribs

Our oldest son always asked for this for his birthday, he loved them since he was very young. We call them "dinosaur bones". They are very messy and delicious- you are going to need a lot of napkins!

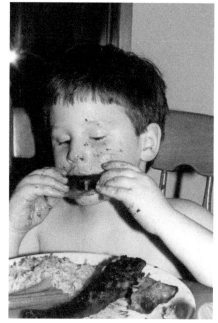

Ingredients:

beef ribs- 2-3 bones per person
John's BBQ Sauce (see recipe)

Directions:

Prepare grill, then heat to very hot- about 500 degrees (F). Meanwhile, prepare the ribs by removing the silverskin or membrane as you would pork ribs. Cut the ribs into single rib sections, and coat with BBQ sauce.

When the grill is ready, put all of the ribs on the grill. After 2 minutes on a side, flip to a new side, and brush the cooked side with sauce. Keep brushing and flipping until done. Since beef ribs tend to have some fat, take care to not let them catch on fire. The total grilling time is about 20-22 minutes for ribs done medium-rare. Beef ribs take longer than steaks because they are bone-in and because you have to open the BBQ lid frequently to baste with sauce. The temperature in the BBQ will reduce, especially in cold weather.

If well-done ribs or fall-off-the-bone ribs are desired, bake in the oven before grilling. Place ribs in a baking pan in a single layer, and cover with foil. Bake at 350 degrees (F) for about 30 minutes. Discard any fat, and then grill per previous instructions, about 50 minutes to 1 hour total cooking time.

Pork Chops- Brined and Grilled

Brining the pork ahead of grilling helps ensure they turn out moist. That little bit of char from grilling really adds to this easy main dish. We like to serve these grilled chops with Savory Plum Sauce (see recipe below). Other options include seasoning the chops with spicy Emeril Lagasse's Essence. Serves 4.

Ingredients:

4 thick-cut pork chops or steaks
salt and pepper

Brine:

1/2 gallon water
2 tablespoons sugar
2 tablespoons salt

Directions:

Using a non-reactive bowl, mix together the brine ingredients, and add the pork. Brine for 3-6 hours, or ideally overnight.

Prepare the grill, and heat it to about 500 degrees (F). If the grill is not hot enough, this will not turn out as moist. When ready to grill, discard the brine and rinse the meat pieces off with fresh cold water. With a paper towel, pat it mostly dry, then lightly salt and pepper the meat.

Grill the chops or steaks for 2 minutes, then rotate 90 degrees and cook 2-3 minutes more on the same side to get nice grill marks. Flip them on the other side of the meat, and grill about 2-3 minutes then rotate them again. Continue cooking until the pork is to the desired doneness. Pork loin, especially, is easy to overcook, and it typically does not take quite as long as beef for the same thickness of meat. You can use a thermometer to determine when they are done.

Let them rest covered with foil for about 5 minutes before serving. These are really delicious served with Savory Plum Sauce.

Savory Plum Sauce: Simmer to desired thickness.
3 tablespoons plum jam
1/2 cup chicken broth
1 teaspoon dried thyme

BBQ Pulled Pork

This is a great dish to have when you are feeding a crowd. The pork can be made ahead and warmed in a crock pot or on the stove. It's also great to freeze, makes for a quick dinner to just heat and serve. We like to serve it with slider buns, extra sauce and traditional coleslaw.

Ingredients:

pork shoulder or pork butt, cut into 3/4 to 1 pound pieces.
1/2 cup chicken stock or broth
your favorite BBQ sauce

Directions:

In a very large baking dish, arrange the large pork pieces, fat side up. Add about 1/2 cup chicken broth to the bottom of the pan to ensure it is moist as it starts cooking. You could use water instead of chicken broth. Cover the pan with foil.

Cook at 250 degrees (F) for about 3-4 hours- the time will vary depending on the size of the pork pieces. Cook until you can easily pull the pork using 2 forks. Pull the pork pieces just a little to get large sized pieces. Let it cool in the juices until cool enough to easily handle. As it cools, it will absorb some of the juice back into the meat. Move the pork to a plate or bowl, and discard the juices left in the pan. Return pork to the pan, and pull all of the pork, removing any large fat pieces or gristle. Add sauce and stir. It will take quite a lot of sauce, depending on how much pork there is and how much sauce you like.

At this point, you can package the pork for the freezer, or you can refrigerate it to be used later.

Hearty Chicken Herb Pot Pie

This is the most hearty and delicious way to use left-over chicken or turkey! You could use any veggie with this such as asparagus or broccoli as well. Serves 2-3

Ingredients:

1 1/2 cups chopped, cooked chicken or turkey
1 red potato or fingerlings, diced (optional)
2 1/2 cups chicken stock or broth
1 carrot, sliced
1 celery rib, sliced
4 large mushrooms, diced
1/2 yellow onion, chopped
1 tablespoon dried oregano
1 tablespoon dried thyme
2 bay leaves
1 teaspoon dried sage
salt and freshly ground pepper to taste
pinch of cayenne pepper (optional)
4 tablespoons butter for sautéing
2 tablespoons flour to thicken
puff pastry or pie dough

Directions:

In a medium pot, sauté onion, carrots, and celery in butter until onion is soft, about 6 minutes. In the last minute, sprinkle in the flour, and stir to incorporate. Add chicken broth, herbs, and potatoes, cook for about 6 minutes more. Add mushrooms, and simmer about 2 minutes more. Taste and add more salt and pepper as necessary. Toss in cooked chicken or turkey. Remove bay leaves. Fill oven-proof bowls leaving 1/2 inch room.

Top with puff pastry or pie dough, and bake per instructions for dough, or until brown. Yummy!

Grilled BBQ Chicken or Pork Ribs

Our family has been making this same recipe for years and years. We just love John's BBQ Sauce (See recipe) for BBQ done on the grill. We use 2 different ways to make BBQ chicken on the grill.

 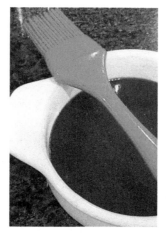 

BBQ Chicken for 2:

If we're cooking for just 2 people, we cook the chicken on the grill before coating it in sauce and finishing it. Begin by cleaning and preparing the grill to very hot (around 500-550 degrees F or more).

Using tongs and a paper towel, oil the grill with high-heat tolerant oil such as avocado oil. Place the chicken bone side down first. This will help the skin side not to stick to the grill. Grill about 2 minutes with the lid closed to get char marks, then rotate the chicken to get more char marks. Once it's charred to the desired amount, flip it and char the other side. When the chicken is charred, turn off one burner and put all of the chicken pieces over the turned off burner for indirect heat. Continue to cook until they are just about cooked through. The cooking time for chicken thighs, for example, will be about 30 minutes total at this high heat.

Turn the grill burner back on, and start coating the pieces in BBQ sauce. Coat all sides and grill on all sides until it has the right amount of caramelization all over. Paint extra sauce on it each time you flip it.

Note: Grilling uncooked skin-on chicken will flame up in the grill. You have to stand by and watch it, and move it out of the flames until all of the fat has cooked off.

BBQ for a crowd:

If we are cooking for a crowd, we like to bake the chicken ahead of time in the oven. Place pieces in a baking dish, skin side up in a single layer and cover with foil. Bake at 350 degrees (F) for about 45-55 minutes, depending on how close together the pieces are in the pan. Cook just short of done since it will cook more on the grill. Drain it, coat it all in sauce, and let it cool. You can do it the day ahead and refrigerate overnight.

When it's grilling time, clean and prepare the grill to very hot. Begin grilling the chicken on all sides until it's got the amount of char and caramelization that you like. Paint extra sauce on it each time you flip it.

If you're making pork ribs, they will need to bake a bit longer than chicken, since they need to get tender as well as cook through. Overcooking them makes them difficult to grill because they want to fall apart. Depending on how many ribs in the pan and whether they are cut into pieces, they will cook covered in foil for about 1 hour. Drain them, and coat them all with sauce. We like to cut ours into about 2-3 rib sections to make grilling easier. But be sure to remove the silverskin or membrane prior to cutting or cooking them.

Spicy Buffalo Chicken Wings- Oven Baked

Serves 3-4

Ingredients:

12 whole chicken wings, separated into pieces
1/2 cup Frank's Hot Sauce
2 tablespoons unsalted butter
1/8 teaspoon cayenne pepper (optional)
freshly ground black pepper to taste
oil for pan (avocado for high heat)

Directions:

Preheat oven to 425 degrees (F).

Use oil and lightly coat a sheet pan or a pan with sides, or you can line a pan with foil (and coat with oil). Place wings in pan skin side up, and bake 25 minutes, or until mostly cooked.

When the chicken is about finished cooking, mix the hot sauce, cayenne, and ground pepper in a small bowl. Melt the butter, and add to the sauce mix. Now it's ready to use.

After wings are mostly cooked, use a large bowl and toss wings in some of the sauce to coat. Return the coated wings to the pan, skin side up. Bake about 8 more minutes, then broil for about 3-5 minutes or until they get a little brown.

Place wings on a serving plate and drizzle remaining sauce over them.

Buffalo Chicken Wraps

Serves 4

Ingredients:

1 1/2 pounds chicken- white or dark meat
broth from cooking the chicken
4 large flour tortillas
1 cup uncooked rice
1/2 cucumber- small diced
1 or 2 celery ribs- diced
blue cheese dressing
blue cheese crumbles (optional)
Frank's Original Buffalo Sauce

Directions:

If using chicken breast, cut the breasts to half thickness, add to a small pan, and cover with water. Bring chicken and water to a boil, and let boil only 30 seconds to 1 minute, and turn the heat off. Let the chicken and water sit for 3 minutes, and then remove chicken to a bowl. Once cool enough to handle, shred the chicken. Spoon 1/4 cup of the hot cooking liquid into the chicken, toss, and set aside. As the chicken cools, it will absorb most of the liquid.

If using dark meat, put in a sauce pan, cover with water. Boil for about 20 minutes, or until the chicken is cooked through. Remove the chicken from the broth. Once cool enough to handle, remove any bones from the chicken and shred. Set chicken aside.

In a rice cooker or sauce pan, cook the rice per the instructions on the package. Instead of adding water, you can add the broth from cooking the chicken (optional).

Once the rice is cooked, warm the chicken, assemble wraps, and serve.

Grilled Lemon Pepper Chicken

Serves 4

Ingredients:

4 chicken pieces (with skin-on)
juice of one lemon
4 tablespoons melted butter
2 teaspoons freshly ground pepper

Directions:

Melt the butter, add the lemon and pepper, and stir. Set aside.

Prepare the chicken by cutting off any fat pieces, leaving the skin intact. Set chicken aside.

Prepare the grill, and then bring back to a very high heat. Grill bone side down first, covered, rotating after a couple of minutes to get grill marks, then flip the chicken, and grill skin side down, covered. Grilling the meat side down helps to oil the grill so when you put the skin side down, it won't stick. You will have to watch it closely, as it can catch on fire as the chicken drips into the fire. Once it has the char and grill marks you like, move to indirect heat in your BBQ, and lower the heat. Let cook, covered, until it's almost done- about 20 minutes total so far.

Start brushing on the lemon mixture, and continue to cook. Flip a few times, brushing as you go. The total cooking time at around 350 degrees (F) will be around 25-30 minutes, depending on the size and cuts you are using. Use a thermometer to verify that the chicken is cooked through.

We like this using chicken thighs. It is also best if the skin gets some char on it. (If you are a skinless chicken person this will probably not be nearly as good, as the charred lemony peppery skin is where it's at!)

Also, we like to make extra lemon-butter-pepper mixture and set it aside, to serve with rice.

Orange Fennel Chicken

John's mom used to make this all the time. When John started making it, our youngest son always requested it, he just loves it. We like to serve it with cooked rice, which is a great way to use the yummy sauce.

Serves 4

Ingredients:

4 pieces chicken- breasts or thighs
4 cups juice from freshly squeezed oranges
1/2 tablespoon fennel seeds
3/4 cup half and half or heavy cream
pinch of salt
freshly ground black pepper
extra virgin olive oil for frying

Directions:

Pat chicken pieces dry, and season with a little salt and pepper. Heat a frying pan to medium-low heat. Add olive oil. If using chicken with skin, place chicken skin side down to start. Fry until the skin side is deep brown, then flip and fry on the other side until the chicken is cooked through. This should take 15 to 25 minutes total for small thighs and breasts, depending on their size. Once cooked through, transfer to a plate.

Add the orange juice, fennel, a pinch of salt, and some freshly ground black pepper to the frying pan. Bring to a boil; stirring to be sure it doesn't stick to the pan and burn. Simmer on medium-low heat until it has reduced by half. Add the half and half or cream, and bring back to a simmer. Continue simmering until it becomes a nice thick sauce.

Add the chicken back to the pan with the sauce and heat until the chicken is heated through. Serve chicken and sauce with cooked white rice.

Paprika Chicken

John's Aunt Georgie gave us this recipe on 8/3/1989. It was given to her by John's mom. A friend of hers made this dish, and then gave her the recipe in about 1953 in Hell's Kitchen, New York City. It's very simple and yummy!

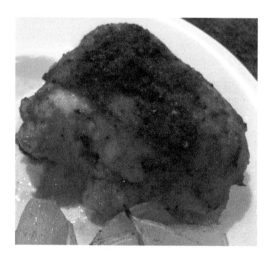

Serves 4

Ingredients:

1 whole chicken, cut into pieces
2 large potatoes, cut into 2" slices
2-3 medium onions, cut into slices or wedges, separated
1 16-ounce can of whole tomatoes
sweet paprika
salt and freshly ground black pepper
extra virgin olive oil

Directions:

Add chicken to a large baking pan. Coat both sides of the chicken with salt, pepper, and a liberal amount of paprika. Tuck slices of potato in between the chicken pieces. Cover with onion pieces. Sprinkle paprika over the vegetables. Dribble olive oil over the top of all of it. Bake in 375 degree (F) oven about 1 to 1 1/2 hours, depending on how close together the pieces are, basting periodically with the juices. Bring chicken to the top to brown at the end.

Crispy Herb Roasted Chicken

Since this chicken is going to be cooked by both baking and broiling, use a pan that is broiler-safe as well as oven-safe. You can use a baking sheet with sides, or a cast iron skillet. We use an enameled cast iron frying pan. Since the oven is so very hot for this recipe, the chicken cooks more quickly than most other baked chicken recipes.

Serves 4

Ingredients:

1 whole chicken cut into pieces- bone in, skin on
1/2 to 1 teaspoon salt (to taste)
1 teaspoon dried thyme
1 teaspoon dried marjoram

1 teaspoon dried rosemary, ground
1 teaspoon baking powder
high heat tolerant oil such as avocado
freshly ground pepper (to taste)

Directions:

Use paper towels to pat the chicken dry. Place the chicken pieces in a dish skin side up. Mix the salt, herbs, baking powder, and pepper together with a little of the oil to make a paste- just thick enough to stay on the chicken. Rub or paint the paste all over the skin side of the chicken. Place in the refrigerator uncovered for 6 to 24 hours.

When it's time to cook, put the top oven rack to the middle of the oven and the bottom rack below that. Place baking/broiling pan on the lower rack of the oven, and preheat the oven and pan to 500 degrees (F). Carefully pull the pan out of the oven, and add chicken skin side down. Since the pan is so hot, it should sizzle quite a bit. Bake the chicken skin side down for 14 minutes, then turn the chicken over, and move to the upper rack and broil skin side up for 5 minutes.

Carefully pull pan out of the oven, and use a thermometer to make sure the chicken is fully cooked, 165 degrees (F) next to the bone. If needed, bake for an additional 5 minutes.

Oven BBQ Chicken

Serves 4

Ingredients:

    chicken thighs and/or breasts- bone in
    1 large yellow onion
    BBQ sauce of your choice

Directions:

Cut onions into large pieces. Sauté them until just starting to soften.

Trim excess fat off the chicken. Pat chicken dry with paper towels. Brush BBQ sauce on both sides of each piece using a basting brush. Place in a large baking pan pieces not touching if possible. Place onion pieces in the spaces between the chicken. Gently pour (I use a spoon to do this) extra sauce over the top of each piece. There will be some sauce in the bottom of the pan as well- all the better.

Bake at 375 degrees (F) for 45 minutes, or if the pan is crowded, it will take longer- maybe 1 hour.

The pan juices go great over rice or pasta.

Duck Breasts with Plum Sauce

This makes a very quick and delicious main dish! We can usually find duck breasts in the frozen meat section of our grocery store. We have on occasion gotten them at a meat shop or an Asian market, but they are typically frozen in any event. While plum sauce is traditional, other fruit jams can be used instead. We make one of 2 different sauces with duck breasts- one is savory, and one is Asian. Both are excellent!

A large branch broke off of our neighbor's plum tree, and we found ourselves in possession of a large bag of plums. So we pitted and blanched the plums to remove the skins, and boiled them with a little sugar and made our own plum jam- it worked perfectly for this recipe.

Ingredients:
  4 duck breasts, boneless, skin on
  oil for frying
  salt and freshly ground pepper

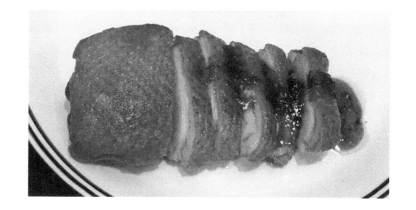

Savory Plum Sauce:
  3 tablespoons plum jam
  1/2 cup chicken stock or broth
  1 teaspoon thyme

Asian Plum Sauce:
  1/2 cup plum jam
  2 teaspoons rice vinegar
  1/2 tablespoon finely minced onion
  1/4 teaspoon grated fresh ginger
  1/2 teaspoon finely minced garlic
  1/8 teaspoon red pepper flakes
  small pinch of 5 spice powder

Directions:

Sprinkle a little salt and pepper on each breast. Fry the duck breasts skin side down first on medium heat until deep golden brown, about 10 minutes. Flip them over, and fry about 5-7 more minutes, or to desired doneness. We like ours done between medium and medium rare. Move them to a plate, and let them rest.

Drain most of the fat from the frying pan. Turn to medium heat, and add the sauce ingredients, scraping any brown bits from the pan into the sauce. Simmer until reduced to desired thickness. Serve the sauce on the side.

Grilled Chicken Under a Brick

Chicken under a brick is typically done using a whole chicken which is spatchcocked (split open) in order to grill it flat and have it be a fairly consistent thickness for even cooking. But this great method can be used for half a chicken as well, just halve the ingredients. The very large chickens are more difficult to cook using this method because they can be so thick. A medium or smaller size is recommended.

We use any number of seasonings for this dish such as Greek Seasoning (see recipe), a Southwest seasoning, garlic and paprika, or the lemon-herb shown below.

Ingredients:

- 1 whole chicken
- 1 cup olive oil
- 4 tablespoons juice from lemon
- 2 tablespoon dried oregano
- 2 tablespoon dried thyme
- 2 tablespoon dried rosemary- ground medium
- 1 teaspoon freshly ground pepper
- 1/2 teaspoon kosher salt

Prepare the chicken: To spatchcock, or split open the chicken, cut along both sides of the backbone and remove it. Turn the bird over to see the inside of the breast area. For 1/2 chicken, cut in-between the breasts. For a whole chicken, don't cut, but use a knife to score the small bone portion of the breast. Turn the bird to skin side up, then using your hands, press to break and flatten between the breast pieces. Tuck the wing tips behind the joint of the wing that meets the breast.

Brine the chicken: In a very large non-reactive bowl, mix 4-6 cups water with 3-4 tablespoons salt and 1/2 teaspoon peppercorns, until the salt is dissolved. Add chicken to bowl, and be sure it's covered with the brine. Let sit refrigerated for 6 hours. When ready, remove the chicken from the brine, rinse it with cold water, and then pat it dry with paper towels.

Mix the seasoning: mix together seasoning ingredients in a small bowl at least 1 hour prior to using to let the flavors mix.

Prepare the grill: clean grill, then bring temperature back up to very hot- around 500 degrees (F). Wrap 2 bricks (or 1 brick for 1/2 chicken) with aluminum foil, and preheat the bricks in the hot BBQ for 20 minutes.

Grill the chicken: Grill bone side down first, covered, and with the bricks on top to help flatten it to the grill. Rotate after a couple of minutes to get grill marks, then flip the chicken and grill skin side down, covered, and with the bricks on top. Grilling the meat side down helps to oil the grill so when you put the skin side down, it won't stick. You will have to watch it closely, as it can catch on fire as chicken fat drips into the fire. Once it has the char and grill marks you like, put the bricks aside and move the chicken to indirect heat in your BBQ and lower the heat. Let cook, covered, until it's almost done- about 15 to 20 minutes total so far.

Start brushing on the lemon-herb mixture and continue to cook. Flip a few times, brushing as you go. The total cooking time at around 350 degrees (F) will be around 30 to 40 minutes, depending on the level of heat in the BBQ and the size of the chicken. Use a thermometer to verify that the chicken is cooked through- 165 degrees (F) near the bone. The preheated brick on top while it chars helps it to cook more quickly than most methods, so using a thermometer is a key to ensuring it does not overcook.

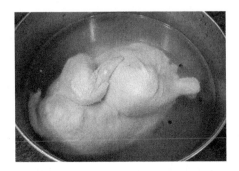

Brined Roasted Stuffed Turkey

Between brining and roasting it covered in foil, this turkey turns out very moist. John's turkey is simply delicious!

Ingredients:

17 pound turkey
brine mix
1/2 stick melted butter
your favorite stuffing

Brine:

3/4 cup salt
3/4 cup brown sugar
2 gallons water
1 yellow onion cut into pieces
1 teaspoon thyme
1 teaspoon marjoram
1 teaspoon oregano
4 bay leaves

Directions:

Brine in a non-reactive pot or cooler, refrigerated, for about 24 hours before time to prepare and stuff the turkey. We use a very large stainless pan (canning pot) with lid. Then we put the pot inside a plastic bin, and put ice around the outside of the pot to keep it cold. Nothing that size will fit in our fridge!

Prepare and Bake Turkey: Preheat oven to 450 degrees (F). Rinse brine off of the turkey and pat dry. Melt a stick of butter, and paint butter over the entire bird skin. Stuff the turkey with your favorite stuffing. We use John's Fresh Herb Stuffing (see recipe).

Place the turkey in the roasting pan breast side up. Truss the legs and wings inward using kitchen string to keep them from drying out. Use some a pins to close the flap of skin over the dressing. Prepare a piece of foil large enough to cover the bird in a tented fashion. If using 2 pieces of foil- be sure they are folded together such that air doesn't escape thru the seam. Coat the shiny side of foil with oil, to prevent it from sticking to the skin. Cover the bird, tenting the foil to touch as little skin as possible. Some will touch- and that's OK.

For a 17 pound turkey, cook covered with foil 2 hours and 40 minutes. Remove the foil, baste it with the cooking juices, and cook uncovered for 25 more minutes. Check that the internal temperature of the bird is at least 165 degrees (F). Remove from heat, cover back up with foil, and let the bird rest for 20 minutes before carving. Adjust the times for a larger or smaller bird. Our 22 pound turkey took 3-1/2 hours cooking time total.

Caution: A brined turkey will produce a lot of liquid in the bottom of the pan. If the turkey is really big for the size of the pan, you may need to drain some juice off half way through the cooking process.

Seafood

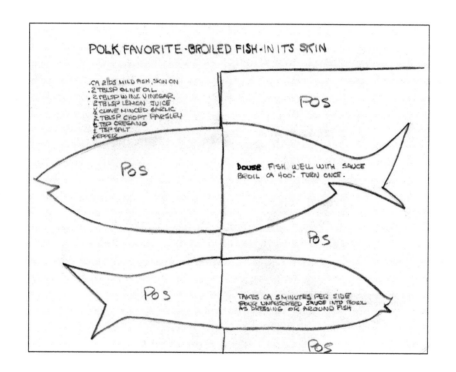

POLK FAVORITE · BROILED FISH · IN ITS SKIN

. CA 2 lbs MILD FISH, SKIN ON
. 2 TBLSP OLIVE OIL
. 2 TBLSP WINE VINEGAR
. 2 TBLSP LEMON JUICE
. ½ CLOVE MINCED GARLIC
. 2 TBLSP CHOPT PARSLEY
. ½ TSP OREGANO
. ½ TSP SALT
. + PEPPER

POS

POS

DOUSE FISH WELL WITH SAUCE
BROIL CA 400° TURN ONCE.

POS

POS

TAKES CA 5 MINUTES PER SIDE
POUR UNFINISHED SAUCE INTO BOWL
AS DRESSING OR AROUND FISH

POS

Jambalaya

Serves 4

Ingredients:

1 cup rice
8 ounces ham chopped
8 ounces andouille sausage chopped
1/2 pound raw prawns
-or- can use dark chicken meat
3/4 cup yellow onion, diced
3/4 cup celery ribs, diced
3/4 cup fresh red pepper, diced
1 large clove garlic, finely minced
1 large jalapeño, seeded and chopped
2 cups chicken stock or broth
3/4 cup water, or additional chicken stock

2 tablespoons tomato paste
8 ounces of diced canned tomatoes
2 bay leaves
1 teaspoon dried oregano
1 teaspoon dried thyme
1 teaspoon paprika (1/2 spicy, 1/2 regular- optional)
1/4 teaspoon freshly ground pepper, or to taste
1/4 teaspoon salt, or to taste
1/4 teaspoon Tabasco hot sauce, or to taste
1 tablespoon butter
extra virgin olive oil for frying
3 chopped green onions, or parsley for garnish

Directions:

Peel and de-vein the prawns, and chop into large pieces. Set aside.

Use a large sauté pan or skillet with high sides. Heat pan to medium, and add oil and butter. Caramelize ham and andouille sausage, and move to a plate. Add onions, red peppers, celery, garlic, and jalapeños to the pan, and sauté until soft. Add canned tomatoes, paste, broth and water, spices and herbs, and the cooked meats. Bring to a boil. Add rice and Tabasco and stir. Bring back to a boil, stir. and cooked covered for 18 minutes. Stir in prawns, and cover and cook 7 more minutes, until rice and prawns are done.

Turn off heat and let sit for 5-7 minutes before serving. Serve garnished with chopped green onions and/or parsley.

Gumbo

John's gumbo is truly delicious. Gumbo should be made using what ingredients are on hand (except we always use crab), as this is a stew and really has many variations. Some steps and some ingredients are necessary to make it turn out right, and hopefully this recipe will explain these. Note that this will take 2-3 hours to prepare and 1-2 hours to cook. We recommend that you get a little help from your friends!

Serves 4

Ingredients:

1 whole Dungeness crab- cooked and cooled

1/2 pound raw shrimp

1/2 pound stewing beef, cut into ¾ inch cubes

1/2 pound chicken- whole dark meat pieces

1 ham bone

1/2 pound ham, diced

2 strips thick-cut bacon, chopped

1/2 pound andouille sausage- sliced

1 cup diced yellow onion

3 green onions, chopped

2 cloves garlic, minced

2-3 ribs celery chopped (including leaves)

2 tablespoons chopped parsley

1 16-ounce can diced tomatoes

2 tablespoons filé (pronounced fee-lay)

1-2 tablespoons Worcestershire sauce

1 teaspoon thyme

up to 1 teaspoon cayenne pepper (spicy!)

2 bay leaves

1/2 teaspoon fresh ground pepper

salt to taste

6-8 tablespoons butter

4 tablespoons flour

Tabasco sauce to taste (add at the end)

seafood stock (see recipe below)

Directions:

About the crab: You can make gumbo with lobster or only shrimp but it would not be the same. Don't use king crab if you can help it, as using the shells for the stock is an absolute must, and the king crab shells don't give as much flavor. It's the body shells that are the big flavor giver. If you can get live crab, that is best. Steam the crabs and reserve the steaming liquid to use in the gumbo. If you can only get cooked crab, no worries but you need the body shells - don't get cleaned crab or just the leg pieces with the knuckles.

Clean the cooked and cooled crab, reserving the shells. Remove meat from the legs and knuckles, and set the meat aside. Separate the crab you clean into 2 piles, one pile with the big pieces which you should set aside for serving, the other pile of remaining crab meat (small pieces) will go into the stew during final assembly. Set both piles of crab aside.

Break shells into pieces, and throw into a pot to be boiled. You will find when you open the body there are bits of white crab fat, mostly in the body cavity. Between the knuckles there is often green stuff, which is the liver. This adds considerable amount of flavor to your stew. Collect as much as you can and toss into the pot with the shells. Throw away the guts and feathers (the spongy things attached to the knuckles). Cover the shells with water (around 6 cups), and boil the shells hard for about 15-20 minutes only. The liquid should be greenish and smell like gumbo. Any shells or fish bones from any of the shrimp or other seafood you are using need to go into the pot as well. This is the key to good gumbo along with the roux. Strain the shells off, and reserve the liquid (5 to 6 cups).

Using a hot frying pan with cooking oil, add the chicken pieces and brown. Once the chicken is brown, de-bone and set aside. Add beef cubes, brown and set aside. Add chopped bacon, brown and set aside. Brown the sliced andouille sausage and set aside.

In a separate large pan start a roux. Add 6 tablespoons of butter and melt. Use a whisk or wooden spatula to incorporate flour to the consistency of a thick liquid. Unless you are willing to stand over it, do this over low heat. If the heat is higher, stir almost constantly. If the flame is low, stir every minute or so, and cook until the roux is a dark chocolate brown. Having a dark brown roux is important to the flavor.

Add onion, celery, garlic, and green onions, and cook until soft, adding more butter if needed to keep the veggies moist. It will take at least 10 minutes or so. Add all the spices, herbs, the liquid, the browned meats, the ham bone, chopped ham, and about 1/2 of the smaller pieces of crab meat. Reserve the other half of the small pieces until the end of the cooking time, as they would otherwise dissolve in the stew since it will be simmering a long time. Simmer until the meat is tender (1-2 hours). If you are using shrimp, add these at the end of the cooking time along with the small crab pieces. Continue to simmer until the shrimp are fully cooked thru, about 5 minutes. Add the filé (pronounced fee-lay) powder. Taste and add additional salt, pepper, and Tabasco as desired.

Serve with rice and a few large pieces of crab legs. Also serve with extra filé powder on the side.

Crab Cakes

Makes about 4 cakes

Ingredients:

meat from 1 whole fresh cooked Dungeness crab
1/4 cup bread crumbs
2 tablespoons chopped fresh parsley
1 large egg
3 tablespoons mayonnaise
1/2 teaspoon Worcestershire sauce
2 teaspoons fresh lemon juice
small pinch cayenne pepper
1/4 teaspoon freshly ground black pepper
1-2 finely chopped green onions
butter for frying, about 3-5 tablespoons
4 lemon wedges

Directions:

Clean the Dungeness crab, leaving the claw meat and large pieces whole. Mix all ingredients, except the butter and lemon and large crab pieces. At the end of mixing, add the large pieces and gently mix. Form into patties. Sauté in butter on medium-low heat until cooked through and browned. Serve with lemon wedges.

Bacon-Wrapped Scallops or Prawns

This makes a main dish for 4, or a great appetizer for a crowd.

We first ate bacon-wrapped scallops when our kids' Uncle Lee came to visit. He worked at an upscale restaurant in downtown Boston and learned to make them there. We were grilling one night when he was visiting, and he made those for us. We just loved them, and since then have made grilled bacon wrapped shrimp as well as the scallops.

Ingredients:

12 large-size sea scallops
-or- extra-large size raw prawns (or some of each!)
6 pieces of bacon (not thick cut)
12 toothpicks
Cocktail Sauce for serving (see recipe)

Directions:

Shell and de-vein the prawns if using.

If the scallops or prawns are smaller, partially cooking the bacon can help make sure the seafood is not overdone before the bacon gets crisp. Cut each slice of bacon into 2 pieces. Wrap one bacon piece around each scallop or prawn, and use a toothpick to secure it.

Preheat broiler or prepare grill.

If using a broiler, put the prawns or scallops on a baking sheet, and broil until the bacon is brown, and the prawns are cooked through, turning them over once. You may need to move them around a little to ensure they all cook evenly. They should only take about 6 or 8 minutes.

If using the grill, place them directly on the grill once it is cleaned and reheated. Cook them until the prawns or scallops are cooked through and the bacon is browned. The time will vary depending on how hot your grill is, but it won't take long at all, so watch them closely.

Shrimp Scampi

Serves 2

Ingredients:

1 1/2 pounds shrimp, peeled and de-veined
salt and freshly ground black pepper
extra virgin olive oil
1/3 to 1/2 cup garlic, chopped (not fine chop)
juice from 3/4 lemon
1/2 cup white wine

2 cups shrimp stock (see recipe below)
5 tablespoons cold butter
2 tablespoons chopped fresh parsley
lemon wedges for garnish
cooked rice

Directions:

Peel shrimp, and use shells to make shrimp stock. Add shells and 2 1/2 cups of water to sauce pan, and boil for 15-20 minutes. Set stock aside.

Season the shrimp thoroughly with salt and pepper. Heat a large sauté pan over medium heat. When the pan is hot, add enough oil to lightly coat the pan. Add the shrimp, and quickly sauté until just starting to turn pink, but not cooked through. Remove from the pan and set aside. Add the garlic, and cook 2-3 minutes, but do not brown. Add the lemon juice, white wine, and stock, and reduce by 2/3, about 15 minutes. Add the shrimp back to the pan, and add the butter. Finish with the parsley, and check for seasoning. Garnish with lemon wedges, and serve over rice.

For a spicy version, add 2 tablespoons paprika and 1/2 teaspoon cayenne. Yum!

Fried Shrimp

Serves 3-4

Ingredients:

1 1/4 pounds large shrimp
1 cup flour
1 teaspoon cayenne pepper (optional)
1/4 teaspoon salt and pepper
1 cup panko crumbs
2 eggs, lightly beaten
1/4 cup milk
1 tablespoon hot pepper sauce
peanut oil for frying

Directions:

Peel and de-vein the shrimp, leaving the tails on. Pat shrimp dry and set aside.

Put about an inch of oil in a small sauce pan. Heat the oil to medium, about 350 degrees (F).

Lightly beat eggs in a medium sized bowl. Add milk and hot sauce. Mix flour, cayenne, salt, and pepper in another bowl. Put panko crumbs in a third bowl. Dredge shrimp in flour, shake off excess. Dip shrimp into egg, then press shrimp into panko. Turn shrimp over, and press into panko again to coat both sides. Transfer to a plate.

Add the shrimp to the hot oil a few at a time, and cook for about 1-2 minutes, until cooked through. Transfer to a clean plate with paper towels. Serve with Tartar Sauce, Cocktail Sauce (see recipes), and lemon wedges on the side.

Instead of using a plate with paper towels to drain, they can be transferred to a rack set on a baking sheet, and then transferred to a 225 degree (F) oven to keep hot for a few minutes until ready to serve.

Salmon- Oven Roasted or Pan Fried

It depends on how big of a piece of fish is as to whether roast it in the oven or just pan fry it. If it's a fillet piece, it's easiest to just cut it into portion sizes and pan fry it. If it's a whole small fish, we like to roast it in the oven.

Ingredients:

1 whole small salmon, around 2 pounds
-or- fillets cut into portion sizes
1 lemon
Tartar Sauce for serving (see recipe)

several sprigs of parsley or dill
(for roasted salmon)
1-2 tablespoons butter
salt and freshly ground pepper

Directions: Oven Roasted Whole Salmon

Clean, scale, rinse the fish, and then pat dry. Place a large piece of foil on a baking sheet with sides. Place the fish on the sheet. Sprinkle a little salt if desired and freshly ground pepper into the cavity of the fish. Slice thin about 1/3 of the lemon. Place pats of butter, along with lemon slices and parsley or dill into the fish cavity. Use olive oil and oil the top skin of the fish. Bake at 350 degrees (F) for about 30 minutes. The time will vary depending on the thickness of the fish. The best way to tell if it's done is to make a small cut into the backbone area of the flesh and check to see if it's cooked to your desired doneness. We like ours still a little translucent in the very center of the flakes. Remove the skin; discard the lemon slices and herb sprigs. Serve with lemon wedges and Tartar Sauce (see recipe).

Pan Fried

Heat a non-stick frying pan to medium heat. Salt and pepper both sides of the fish. Add butter to the pan, and immediately add the salmon pieces. Fry until the middle is still translucent, and the bottom looks done. Flip it over, and continue to fry to the desired doneness. When it's close to done, the flakes will separate a little. This allows you to get a peek at how done it is. Serve with lemon wedges and T's Tartar Sauce (see recipe).

Steamed Clams

As a main dish, 4 pounds of clams is enough for 2 people. As an appetizer, 4 pounds will serve about 4.

Ingredients:

> 4 pounds live manila clams
> 1/4 cup dry white wine
> 2 tablespoons finely chopped shallot
> water enough to fill 1/2 inch in the pan
> extra virgin olive oil
> 2 tablespoons chopped parsley to garnish

Directions:

Rinse the clams with cold water. For any clams that are slightly open, if they are still alive, when you tap them they will close up. Discard any that are not fully closed.

Heat a large pan to medium. Add the oil, and sauté the shallots. Add the wine and water. Bring back to a boil. Add the clams, and cover to steam.

The clams are done when they are all open, around 5-7 minutes. Discard any that do not open while cooking.

Spaghetti with Clams

Serves 4

Ingredients:

5 pounds fresh clams
10 ounces clam juice,
1 pound spaghetti pasta
1/4 cup dry white wine
1 1/2 tablespoons olive oil

2-3 tablespoons butter
1 tablespoons fresh oregano, finely chopped
4 tablespoons shallot or sweet onion, minced
2 teaspoons finely chopped garlic
2 tablespoons fresh parsley, finely chopped

Directions:

Cook spaghetti pasta per the instructions on the package. Drain water from the pasta.

Rinse the clams with cold water. For any clams that are slightly open, if they are still alive, when you tap them they will close up. Discard any that are not fully closed.

Put butter and olive oil in a large pot with a lid. Sauté shallots and/or onions uncovered in the oil and butter until onions are soft. Add garlic, and cook for about 1 minute. Add clam juice and wine, and let come to a boil. Add oregano and clams. Cover and let steam for about 5-7 minutes until clams all open.

Once the clams are fully cooked, add the clams and sauce to the pasta in a serving bowl. Be sure to discard any clams that did not open.

Garnish with the fresh parsley, and serve with some nice rustic bread.

Mexican

Carne Asada

Serves 4

Ingredients:

2 pounds skirt steak (or can use flank)
1 tablespoon garlic, grated
1/4 onion- sliced
juice of 2 limes
juice of 2 oranges

1/2 cup extra-virgin olive oil
1 tablespoon chili powder
1/2 teaspoon cumin
pinch salt and pepper to taste
1/4 cup chopped cilantro

Directions:

Make marinade by mixing all of the above ingredients together. Cut steak into large pieces, and marinate overnight.

Prepare BBQ, and bring back to very hot (around 500 degrees (F). Shake off excess marinade, and grill to desired doneness for steak. Let rest for 5-8 minutes before cutting into strips across the grain.

This is excellent for tacos or fajitas.

For fajitas, use a frying pan and a little olive oil, and sauté red and/or green peppers along with onions. If desired, you can also grill green onions and jalapeños. Just brush with a little olive oil and grill along side steak. Serve meat, peppers, and onions, with flour or corn tortillas. Garnish with cheese, salsa, sour cream, and guacamole.

Enchiladas

Enchiladas can be different every time you make them. We love them with ground beef, chicken, or Carnitas (shredded Mexican pork- see recipe). Serves 4

Ingredients:

12 corn tortillas
1 pound of ground beef or chicken breast
Mexi-Mix Seasoning (see recipe)
salt to taste
1/2 pound cheddar cheese
1/2 yellow onion, chopped
Homemade Enchilada Sauce (see recipe)
-or- can use 1 28-ounce can as desired
sliced black olives (optional)
chopped green chilis (optional)

Directions:

For ground beef enchiladas, brown the beef and drain off any excess fat. Season the meat with Mexi-Mix Seasoning and salt to taste. Add 1-2 tablespoons water and mix. Set aside.

For chicken enchiladas, cut the breasts to half thickness, add to a small pan, and cover with water. Bring chicken and water to a boil, and let boil only 30 seconds to 1 minute, and turn the heat off. Let the chicken and water sit for 3 minutes, and then remove chicken to a bowl. Once cool enough to handle, shred the chicken. Spoon 1/4 cup of the hot cooking liquid into the chicken, toss, and set aside. As the chicken cools, it will absorb most of the liquid. Drain the chicken if needed, and season with Mexi-Mix Seasoning to taste and set aside.

Heat a fry pan to medium heat. Add a small amount of oil to the pan. Add 1 tortilla at a time and cook on both sides until it starts to cook and it softens. Pull off the heat, and fill it with meat and any other filling you are using. Roll it and place in a large baking dish, seam side down. Do this for the rest. It's OK for the enchys to touch each other. Once the pan is full, pour enchilada sauce over the entire batch. Sprinkle grated cheddar cheese on top of the sauce, and bake in a 350 degree (F) oven until heated through, about 30 minutes.

If making enchiladas ahead for a gathering, prepare everything the same up to the point of pouring the enchilada sauce on. If you do this too early, the tortillas will get soggy. Reserve some cheese to put over the top before putting into the oven. They may take a bit longer to cook if the filling is cold when they go into the oven. Your guests are going to love them!

Tamales

John has been making tamales for years and years. For the filling, we use seasoned ground beef or chicken. We also sometimes use Carnitas or Mexican Pork (see recipes). For a vegetarian option, you could use a roasted red and poblano peppers and corn medley as the filling. Serves 3-4

Ingredients:

3/4 pound ground beef or chicken breast
Mexi-Mix Seasoning (see recipe)
2 cups masa
2/3 cup lard or Crisco shortening
1 1/2 to 2 cups chicken stock or broth
2 teaspoons baking powder
pinch of salt

1 ear fresh corn on the cob (optional)
dried corn husks
toothpicks
Homemade Enchilada Sauce (see recipe)
-or- canned as desired
cheddar cheese, grated

Directions:

For ground beef tamales, brown the beef, and drain off any excess fat. Season the meat with Mexi-Mix Seasoning and salt to taste. Add 1-2 tablespoons water and mix. Set aside.

For chicken tamales, cut the breasts to half thickness, add to a small pan, and cover with water. Bring chicken and water to a boil, and let boil only 30 seconds to 1 minute, and turn the heat off. Let the chicken and water sit for 3 minutes, and then remove chicken to a bowl. Once cool enough to handle, shred the chicken. Spoon 1/4 cup of the hot cooking liquid into the chicken, toss, and set aside. As the chicken cools, it will absorb most of the liquid. Drain the chicken if needed, and season with Mexi-Mix Seasoning to taste and set aside.

95

In a large bowl, cover the dried corn husks with hot tap water to soak. Set aside. Shuck the corn and cut all the kernels off the cob and set aside.

Use a mixer and beat the shortening first. Add and mix 1 cup masa, 1 teaspoon baking powder, and a pinch of salt, scraping the sides as you go. Once fully incorporated, add the 2nd cup of masa and the 2nd teaspoon of baking powder, and continue to beat until about the consistency of course sand. Scrape any remaining liquid from the corn cob into the masa mix.

Add 1 cup of chicken broth, and beat the masa mix. Add broth a little at a time and mix, until it becomes quite loose, but not soupy- about 1 1/2 to 2 cups total broth. Let rest for 3 to 5 minutes. Add a little broth to adjust the consistency if needed. It will tighten up as it sits. When you spread the masa on the corn husks, it should spread on super easy but not be runny- maybe like the consistency of loose hummus.

Once the masa mix is the right consistency, add the corn kernels and gently stir them in. Drain the corn husks. Use the back of a spatula and apply a liberal amount of dough in the middle of a corn husk. Spread it out over the sides and bottom and within an inch or so of the top of the husk, and add a couple of tablespoons filling to the middle of the dough.   Wrap the corn husk up so the dough surrounds the filling. Fold the husks up at the bottom, and secure them closed using toothpicks. Leave open at the top. Gently squeeze the tamale closed at the top. If the dough did not cover the filling, just spoon a little dough on top.

Use a steamer basket in a large pot filled with water to the bottom of the steamer basket. Steam the tamales for 45 minutes, checking to be sure there is still water in the bottom of the pan. Remove from heat and steam, and let rest for 5 minutes- they need to rest to fully solidify.

If desired, unwrap some of the tamales and place in a baking pan. Cover with enchilada sauce and cheese. Bake in the oven at 350 degrees (F) until the sauce is bubbly and the cheese is melted. We like to serve some plain still wrapped in the husks, and some enchilada style.

Quesadillas

Serves 4 or more as an appetizer, or 1-2 as a main dish, depending on the size of your tortillas

Ingredients:

1/2 pound ground beef or 1 large chicken breast
2 flour tortillas
oil for frying (olive or avocado)
Mexi–Mix Seasoning (see recipe)
salt to taste
grated cheddar cheese

Sample Garnishes:

sour cream
avocado slices or guacamole
salsa
cilantro leaves
chopped tomatoes
chopped sweet onions

Directions:

Sauté the ground beef until it's cooked through. Drain any excess fat there may be. Add Mexi-Mix Seasoning and salt to taste. If the meat seems a little dry, you can add a tablespoon or two of water and maybe a little more Mexi-Mix Seasoning.

If using chicken breast, cut the breasts to half thickness, add to a small pan, and cover with water. Bring chicken and water to a boil, and let boil only 30 seconds to 1 minute, and turn the heat off. Let the chicken and water sit for 3 minutes, and then remove chicken to a bowl. Once cool enough to handle, shred the chicken. Spoon 1/4 cup of the hot cooking liquid into the chicken, toss, and set aside. As the chicken cools, it will absorb most of the liquid. Drain the chicken if needed, and season with Mexi-Mix Seasoning to taste and set aside.

Heat a non-stick pan to medium low heat. Add a little oil and swirl one tortilla around in it to coat the first side. Add the cheese on top of the tortilla, and then add the meat. Adding the cheese as the first layer helps it stick together better when you go to flip it over. Add any other ingredients you want, and then put the 2nd tortilla on top. Once the cheese if fully melted and the tortilla is brown on the bottom, carefully flip it over to cook on the 2nd side. Put it on a cutting board, and use a pizza cutter or knife to cut into wedges. Garnish with your favorites!

What to put inside a quesadilla is endless- chopped roasted chilis, or pickled jalapeños are some additional ideas. We make ours differently each time!

Carnitas

Ingredients:

2 1/2 to 3 pounds pork butt or shoulder (bone-in or boneless)
2 1/2 to 3 cups beef and/or chicken stock or broth
2 dried guajillo pepper
2 dried ancho pepper
1 whole large yellow onion, coarsely chopped
2-3 cloves garlic
2 jalapeño, seeded
1 teaspoon dried oregano
1/2 teaspoon freshly ground pepper
2 tablespoons Mexi-Mix Seasoning (see recipe)
salt as desired

Directions:

Remove seeds and stems of dried peppers, and tear into large pieces. Cut the pork into several large pieces.

Using a pressure cooker, add the veggies, liquids, spices and herbs. Place the pork pieces on top. Secure the locking lid and heat to medium to get the pressure going. Cook for 45 minutes, and then turn off heat. Allow it to cool, and then once the pressure valve drops; you can carefully open the lid.

Move the pork to a baking pan, reserving the cooking liquid. Let it cool enough to handle, then pull the pork. Remove any gristle or fat pieces and discard. Remove and discard any remaining skins from the peppers. Add any remaining onion pieces to the pulled pork. If the pork seems dry, add some of the cooking liquid to the pan, but use it slowly and taste as you go. The flavors can have intensified. If needed, add broth or water. At this point, you can taste it and see if you'd like to add salt. We find that we don't need to add salt when we're using it with other foods that contain a lot of salt, such as store bought broth or cheese.

If you'd like to get a little browning on top, you can broil the pulled pork; this adds a little extra flavor. When we're using it with something with a lot of ingredients, such as fried burritos, we don't bother with this step. Add a little more broth if needed to get the desired level of moisture.

Mexican Pork

This pork is great used in burritos or tamales. It's different than pork carnitas in consistency as well as flavor, and just as delicious!   Serves 4-5

Ingredients:

    2-3 pound pork loin roast, with fat cap
    1/4 cup Mexi-Mix Seasoning (see recipe)
    1/2 teaspoon cayenne
    1 cup chicken stock or broth
    1/2 teaspoon salt (less if stock is salted)

Directions:

Mix seasonings together, and rub into the meat all over. Wrap meat in plastic wrap, and let sit in the refrigerator for 24 hours.

Preheat oven to 400 degrees (F). Put meat in an oven proof pan. Put 1 cup chicken broth in the bottom of the pan, and cover the pan with foil. Don't pour it over the meat, as it would remove a lot of the spice coating.

Put roast in the oven, and turn the temperature down to 275 degrees (F). Cook for 2 hours.

Remove from oven, and let rest for 20-30 minutes in the pan with the broth and juices. Remove from pan, and remove the fat cap and discard. Cut the entire roast into 1/2 inch cubes, and place in a non-reactive bowl. Add some of the liquid from the pan a few tablespoons at a time, until the meat no longer absorbs more of the liquid.

At this point you can use the pork to make burritos, tamales, tacos, or quesadillas. You can also put portion sizes in the freezer. It freezes cooked very nicely and makes for quick and simple meals!

Fried Burritos

You can put anything you like inside of a burrito, but our favorites are seasoned ground beef, Carnitas, or Mexican Pork (see recipes), as well as cheese. You can put beans inside if desired. Once cooked, garnish with what you have on hand. Serves 2

Ingredients:

- 3/4 pound cooked meat of your choice
- 2 large flour tortillas
- grated cheddar cheese
- oil for frying- avocado or olive oil
- sliced black olives (optional)

Sample Garnishes:

- sour cream
- avocado slices or guacamole
- salsa
- cilantro leaves
- chopped tomatoes
- chopped sweet onions

Directions:

Cook meat. If using ground beef, prepare the same as you would for Enchiladas (see recipe), and set aside.

Assemble the burritos using meat and cheese and sliced black olives if you've got them. Tuck the ends under and roll the burrito closed. Press it somewhat flat to enable cooking on 2 sides.

Heat a frying pan to medium low heat. Add a tablespoon of oil. Place the burritos tortilla flap side down first to get a good seal. Cook until deep brown on each side. Serve immediately with what garnishes you like.

Chili Rellenos

When our oldest son was in college, he called one Saturday night to "ask Dad how to make Chili Rellenos". His buddies were over and they were all starving, and Jay had told them about his Dad's great Mexican food. Because he was in college, he didn't have any modern conveniences such as a mixer, so he improvised and just used a fork to beat the egg whites! He said it took a long time to get the whites stiff, but it turned out delicious! The guys all loved them, and they still talk about that night cooking Mexican food at Jay's apartment.

Our younger son, Tim used to request Chili Rellenos for his birthday dinner- which of course Dad would always make.

Ingredients:

    4 poblano peppers
    3-4 ounces cheddar cheese, sliced or grated
    -or- 3-4 ounces mix of cheddar and queso fresco
    -or- 3-4 ounces mix of jack and cheddar cheeses
    flour
    oil for frying- avocado or olive
    3 extra-large eggs
    Homemade Enchilada Sauce (see recipe)

Directions:

Place the peppers on a sheet pan, and broil until the skin chars on both sides. Be careful to not overcook the peppers. Put the roasted peppers in a plastic bag with about a teaspoon of water, and tie the bag trapping air in it to let the peppers steam until cool. Remove the skin that comes easily off. Don't worry about any skin still on and do not rinse them, this adds flavor. Make one cut lengthwise into each pepper along the side. Remove the seeds, but leave the stem. Move to a paper towel to get any excess moisture off.

101

Stuff each pepper with cheese and fold closed. Dredge each pepper in flour, and pat it to coat the pepper and help seal the cut edges closed. Set aside.

Separate the 3 eggs, using a medium sized mixing bowl for the egg whites. Beat the egg whites until stiff peaks form. In a separate small dish, beat the egg yolks with a fork. Once ready to cook the rellenos, gently fold the yolks into the whites.

Heat a fry pan to medium heat, and add oil for frying. This works best with about 1/8 inch of oil over the whole pan. Once the oil is hot, begin putting egg mixture onto one side of each pepper, and put into the pan, egg side down. Once all of the peppers are in the pan, now spoon some egg mixture on the top of each pepper. Cook until brown on the bottom, and carefully flip them over to cook the egg on the other side. Once brown on both sides, transfer to a plate with paper towels.

Serve immediately with warmed enchilada sauce on top.

Taco Pie

When our kids were growing up, they used to request this for dinner frequently. It's an easy meal that can be put together quickly after a long day out. This is what they requested when their friends were coming over as well. When the oldest went off to college, he made this for his friends, and they loved it! (Hi Lance!)

Ingredients:

1 pound ground beef
1 15-ounce can tomato sauce
Mexi-Mix Seasoning to taste (see recipe)
salt to taste
2 cans crescent rolls (refrigerated Pillsbury)
Fritos Corn Chips
sliced black olives
1 16-ounce container sour cream
8 ounces grated cheddar cheese

Serve With:

salsa
diced fresh tomatoes
diced sweet onions
guacamole or sliced avocados
pickled jalapeños

Directions:

In a saucepan, cook the ground beef until done. Add Mexi-Mix Seasoning and salt to taste. Add tomato sauce and stir. The consistency should be like thick chili.

Using a 9x12 baking dish, lay out the 2 cans of crescent rolls, covering the bottom and sides like a crust. Crush some corn chips onto crescent rolls for texture. Bake crust at 350 degrees (F), until not quite done, but just starting to brown. Do not over-cook, since this will be going back into the oven.

Put ground beef mixture on cooked crust. Dollop the sour cream on top of the ground beef, spreading it as much as possible. Put the grated cheddar on top of the sour cream. Crush more chips on top for more crunchy goodness. Add sliced olives to top.

Bake at 350 degrees (F) until done, about 20 minutes, until the cheese is melted and it is heated through. The sides should look nice and brown. Serve with salsa and veggies.

Chile Verde

Ingredients:

3 pounds pork butt or shoulder
1 yellow onion, sliced thick or wedged
1 pound tomatillos
4 jalapeños + 2 serranos + 4 poblano chilis
5 garlic cloves, peeled
2 tablespoons dried oregano
2 tablespoons ground cumin
salt and pepper to taste
1 1/2 cups chicken stock or broth
masa for thickening

Directions:

If you prefer less spicy chili, use Anaheim chilis instead of the jalapeños, serranos and poblanos.

Trim majority of the fat off the pork butt or shoulder and cut into 1-inch cubes. If using loin (not recommended for this dish), don't trim the fat.

Husk, rinse and halve tomatillos. In a bowl, toss the onions, tomatillos, and garlic with 1 tablespoon olive oil and spread on a baking sheet skin side up. Roast in a 400 degree (F) oven until soft and starting to brown, about 20 to 30 minutes. Let cool and peel skins off. Using a food processor, process vegetables (or simply chop) to a small dice.

Cut all the peppers in half lengthwise and remove seeds and stems. Place on a sheet pan, skin side up, and broil until the skin is blackened almost all over. Put the roasted peppers in a plastic bag with about a teaspoon of water and tie the bag, trapping air in it to let the peppers steam until cool. Remove the skin that comes easily off. Don't worry about any skin still on and do not rinse, this adds flavor. When cool enough to handle, add to the food processor or chop small.

Brown the pork on all sides in a Dutch oven on the stove top. Add seasonings, veggies, and chicken stock. Simmer until pork is tender, approximately 1 1/2 hours. Taste and add salt and pepper if needed. If thicker sauce is desired, at the end add masa to tighten it up (approx. 2 tablespoons).

Serve with fresh tortillas, cilantro, and lime wedges. Other garnishes may include a dollop of sour cream or shredded jack cheese. Freeze in portion sizes for future quick meals.

Red Beef Chili

Serves 4

Ingredients:

1 pound lean ground beef
10-ounce sirloin steak (optional)
3 tablespoons oil for cooking
1 large yellow onion, chopped
1 large rib celery, chopped
3 cloves garlic, minced
2 large jalapeños, seeded and chopped
1/4 cup cilantro stems, chopped
2 poblano peppers
6 tablespoons Mexi-Mix Seasoning (see recipe)
2 bay leaves

12-ounce beer (such as Guiness)
1 cup beef stock or broth
1 28-ounce can crushed tomatoes
1 6-ounce can tomato paste
salt to taste

Suggested Garnishes:

cilantro leaves
grated cheddar cheese
chopped onion
roasted jalapeño slices

Directions:

Roast the poblanos: Cut peppers in half lengthwise and remove seeds and stem. Place the peppers on a sheet pan, skin side up, and broil until the skin is blackened almost all over. Put the roasted peppers in a plastic bag with about a teaspoon of water and tie the bag, trapping air in it to let the pepper steam until cool. Remove the skin that comes easily off. Don't worry about any skin still on and do not rinse, this adds flavor. When cool enough to handle, chop and set aside.

Heat oil, and sauté the vegetables, except the poblanos, until soft. Add the seasonings, and the ground beef. If using ground beef that is not lean, cook in separate pan, drain fat, then add it to the sautéed veggies. Add tomato products, beer, stock or water, roasted poblanos, and bay leaves. Simmer on low heat in uncovered pot for 45 minutes. If it gets too thick, add a little more water as needed. Taste and add salt as needed.

Meanwhile, grill sirloin steak (if using) to rare, and let sit for 10 minutes. Once rested and cooled, cut into bite-sized pieces. Set aside and add to chili during the last 5 minutes of cooking.

Serve with desired garnishes.

Tacos

Using grass-fed beef and fresh tortillas make tacos that much better. You can put any kind of meat in tacos- cooked, shredded, and seasoned chicken (see Enchilada recipe) or chopped Carne Asada (see recipe). Put whatever you like in tacos, and use what you've got on hand. Sometimes we use Pico de Gallo (see recipe) instead of lettuce, tomatoes, and onions. Ours are different every time.

Ingredients:

- lean ground beef
- Mexi-Mix Seasoning (see recipe)
- salt to taste
- corn tortillas
- oil for frying-olive or avocado
- your favorite taco veggies

Sample garnishes:

- cheddar cheese, grated
- sour cream
- taco sauce
- pickled jalapeños
- avocado slices
- cilantro leaves
- black olives

Directions:

Cook the ground beef until fully cooked through in a sauce pan. Drain any excess fat, and add Mexi-Mix Seasoning and salt to taste. If needed, add about 1-2 tablespoons of water to moisten. Set meat aside. Chop, shred, grate, or slice ingredients to be used and put on serving platter.

Heat a large frying pan to medium-low heat. Once hot, add just a little oil to the pan. Once hot, put as many tortillas as will fit in your pan laying flat. Add some meat to each tortilla, and cook on medium-low until the tortillas begin to turn brown on the bottom and the meat is heated through. Using your spatula, fold the tortilla in half, trapping the meat inside. Continue to cook until its light golden brown, and then transfer to a serving plate. Do the same with another batch of tortillas. If using uncooked fresh tortillas, they will need to be cooked a little on the first side before flipping and adding the meat, and then making into tacos.

If making more than just a few tacos, you can make them a few at a time, transfer them to an oven-proof baking pan, and keep them in a 220 degrees (F) oven until all of the tacos are ready to serve.

We have made tacos for a crowd by making them just ahead of people coming over and, putting them in a large baking pan, and then heating them up covered with foil at about 250 degrees (F) for 1/2 hour before serving, uncovering the last 10 minutes. If reheated uncovered, the tortillas can dry out. Reheat any leftover tacos in a frying pan with a tiny bit of oil on low heat. This will crisp them up.

Margaritas

If you're making a Mexican food feast for a crowd, you should consider making homemade margaritas; your guests will love it! You can make the mix ahead, and then add the alcoholic ingredients when you mix the drinks. Margarita Mix will keep in the fridge for up to a couple of weeks. Stir before using. Makes about 6 drinks

Ingredients:

For the Margarita Mix:
    1 cup simple syrup:
        1 cup sugar
        1 cup water
    2/3 cup juice from fresh lime- about 9 limes
    1/3 cup juice from fresh lemon- about 1-2 lemons

For the drinks:
    good quality tequila of your choice
    triple sec
    margarita mix
    lime wedges for garnish
    salt for rims
    lots of ice

Directions:

In a small saucepan, make the simple syrup by mixing the water and sugar and heating until the sugar is dissolved. Set aside to cool while you squeeze juice from lemons and limes. Combine the simple syrup and fruit juices into a pitcher, and refrigerate until time to use. Note: Our family likes less-sweet margaritas, so we use 1/2 of the amount of simple syrup for the amount of juice. Make it to your liking!

For each drink: Use a lime to wet the rim of the glass, and salt the rim if desired, and add below ingredients to a shaker. Pour the margarita into the salted glass, put a lime wedge on the rim, and then serve!

    1 shot (1 1/2 ounces) of tequila
    1 tablespoon triple sec

    2 shots (3 ounces) of margarita mix
    plenty of ice

Alternately, you can mix a whole pitcher of already made drinks to the same proportion as a single drink. Just add ice to the glasses and pour the tequila/juice mix on top and garnish. This works well if you're serving a large crowd and using multiple recipes of the Margarita Mix.

Asian

Kung Pao Chicken

Serves 2

Ingredients:

3/4 pound skinless boneless chicken thighs
4 tablespoons minced fresh garlic
4 tablespoons minced fresh ginger
1 teaspoon low-sodium soy sauce
4 teaspoons Shaoxing rice wine
2 tablespoons chicken stock or broth
1 tablespoon balsamic vinegar
1 1/2 teaspoons dark soy sauce
3/4 cup peanuts, roughly chopped
1 teaspoon corn starch or arrowroot powder

1 teaspoon sesame oil
2 tablespoons peanut oil
5 or 6 dried Thai red chilis, seeds removed
-or- can use 1 teaspoon chili garlic paste
1/2 to 1 red bell pepper, cut into 1-inch pieces
6-7 asparagus spears, cut into 2 inch pieces
-or- can use bok choi, snow peas, etc.
1/2 cup green onions- white parts separated
cooked rice for serving

Directions:

Cut the chicken into 1/2 inch cubes. In a bowl, combine the chicken, low-sodium soy sauce, 1 teaspoon water, and 1 teaspoon of rice wine. Let chicken marinate while you prepare the rest. In a separate bowl or jar, combine the chicken broth, chili garlic paste (if using), balsamic vinegar, sesame oil, dark soy, corn starch, and 3 teaspoons rice wine. Set aside.

Heat a large wok over medium heat. Once hot, add oil then wait until it's hot, and add chicken. Spread out chicken on the bottom and sides of wok and let sear for about 1 minute. Stir-fry until cooked through. Remove the meat and place in a dish.

Let the wok heat up again, and then add another tablespoon of oil. Stir fry peppers, asparagus, bok choi or snow peas, chilis (if using), and green onion white parts until not quite done. Add the garlic and ginger, and stir fry for about another minute. At the very end; throw in the chicken, sauce, and then the green onion green parts. Stir fry until everything is heated. The vegetables should still be crunchy, not cooked through.

Remove from heat and stir in peanuts. Serve immediately with cooked rice.

Mongolian Beef Stir Fry

You can use any veggies you have on hand for this stir fry.   We like asparagus, red peppers, broccoli, mushrooms, and green onions. Serve with cooked rice or rice noodles.   Serves 2

Ingredients:

1 pound beef sirloin steak
2 tablespoons minced garlic
2 tablespoons minced ginger
3 green onions
6 tablespoons low-sodium soy sauce
2 teaspoons dark soy sauce
1 teaspoon brown sugar
2 teaspoons corn starch

2 tablespoons Shaoxing rice wine
2 tablespoons hoisin sauce
1 tablespoon rice vinegar
2 teaspoons chili garlic sauce
1-3 teaspoons red chili flakes (to taste)
veggies to stir fry, cut into pieces
oil for stir frying -peanut or avocado

Directions:

Combine the liquid ingredients plus the cornstarch, brown sugar, and chili flakes, into a jar with a lid, and shake to mix. Set aside. Cut the beef into strips across the grain. Cut the green onions, separating the green parts from the white. Cut whatever you are using veggies into about 1" pieces for stir frying.

Heat a large wok over medium heat. Once hot, add oil then wait until it's hot, and add meat. Spread out meat on the bottom and sides of wok, and let sear for about 1 minute. Stir-fry until cooked to desired level. Remove the meat, and place in a dish.

Let the wok heat up again, and then add another tablespoon of oil. Stir fry the firmer vegetables including the white parts of the green onions until not quite done. Then add the garlic and ginger and any softer vegetables, and stir fry for about another minute, until cooked almost done. At the very end add the meat and sauce into the wok, and stir fry until everything is heated through. The vegetables should be crunchy, not cooked through.

If using rice noodles, add about 3 tablespoons water to the stir fry. They soak up liquid, so you'll want a little extra sauce. When completely heated through, add the rice noodles and stir until noodles are soft. Serve immediately. Garnish with the green parts of the onions.

Stir Fry with Rice Noodles

This noodle dish can be made with any meat or veggies you have on hand. We typically use veggies like asparagus, bok choi, sliced carrots, green onions, sometimes mushrooms. It's different every time! The dark soy gives it the darker color (and added flavor) than other stir frys.   Serves 4

Ingredients:

1 to 1 1/2 pounds beef or pork sirloin
-or- 2 large boneless chicken thighs
1/2 cup rough-chopped garlic
1/2 cup rough-chopped ginger
2/3 pound rice noodles
oil for stir frying-peanut or avocado
vegetables to stir fry

Sauce:

1 teaspoon dark soy sauce
3 tablespoons low-sodium soy sauce
1 1/2 cups chicken stock or broth
2 tablespoons mirin
5 tablespoons Shaoxing rice wine
2 tablespoons chili garlic sauce, to taste (spicy!)

Directions:

Cut the meat into strips across the grain, into bite-sized pieces. Add 1 tablespoon low-sodium soy and let marinate in a small bowl for 1 hour. Combine all of the sauce ingredients and set aside. Soak noodles covered in hot tap water for at least 15 minutes prior to using.

Heat a large wok over medium heat. Once hot, add oil then wait until it's hot, and add meat. Spread out meat on the bottom and sides of wok, and let sear for about 1 minute, then stir-fry until cooked to desired level, but chicken should be cooked through. Remove the meat to a dish.

Let the wok heat up again, and then add another tablespoon of oil. Stir fry the firmer vegetables including the white parts of the green onions until not quite done. Then add the garlic, ginger, and any softer vegetables, and stir fry for about another minute, until cooked almost done. At the very end; add the meat and sauce into the wok, and stir fry until everything is heated through. The vegetables should be crunchy, not cooked through.

Once the veggies are cooked to desired level, drain the rice noodles, and add them to the stir fry. Continue stir frying until the noodles, meat and veggies are heated through and the noodles are soft. Serve immediately.

Simple Stir Fry

What goes into a stir fry depends on what you have in the house. There are a wide variety of meats, veggies and sauces that make it yummy. The sauce typically has 1 sweet element like hoisin or teriyaki, and 1 hot element (if spicy is desired). This added to chicken broth and corn starch makes a very simple sauce.   Serves 2

Ingredients:

3/4-1 pound pork loin or sirloin steak
-or- 1 chicken breast or can use shrimp
2 tablespoons low-sodium soy sauce
1 carrot, sliced thin
1/2 pound asparagus, cut into 1 inch pieces
2 green onions, chopped
1 1/2 to 2 cups Napa cabbage
-or- bok choy, roughly chopped
1 1/2 cup coarsely chopped mushrooms
2 tablespoon freshly grated ginger
2 tablespoon finely minced garlic
oil for stir frying (avocado or peanut)
1/2 teaspoon sesame oil

Stir Fry Sauce:

3 tablespoons Hoisin sauce
-or- teriyaki stir- fry sauce
1 tablespoon soy sauce
1/4 cup spicy Szechuan sauce (for spicy)
-or- Thai peppers if desired.
1/2 cup chicken stock or broth
1/2 teaspoon corn starch

Directions:

Cut meat into 1/8 inch thick strips across the grain, and marinate in 2 tablespoons soy sauce about an hour. Mix the sauce ingredients in a jar and set aside.

Heat a large wok over medium heat. Once hot, add oil, then wait until it's hot, and add meat. Spread out meat on the bottom and sides of wok, and let sear for about 1 minute. Stir-fry until cooked to desired level, but chicken should be cooked through. Remove the meat, and place in a dish.

Let the wok heat up again, and then add another tablespoon of oil. Stir fry the firmer vegetables including the white parts of the green onions until not quite done. Add the garlic, ginger, and any softer vegetables and stir fry for about another minute, until cooked 'almost' done. At the very end; add the meat, sauce, and sesame oil into the wok and stir fry until everything is heated through. The vegetables should be crunchy, not cooked through. Serve with rice or rice noodles. If using rice noodles, you may want to add 3 tablespoons of water in the end as required.

Grilled Teriyaki Chicken/Pork/Beef

Ingredients:

2 pounds boneless chicken- breasts or thighs
-or- 2 pounds of pork loin
-or- 2 pounds of beef sirloin
teriyaki sauce (see recipe)
cooked rice for serving

Sauce: (makes approx. 2 cups)

1 1/3 cups mirin (Japanese sweet rice wine)
2 cups low-sodium soy sauce
9 teaspoons rice vinegar
2 teaspoons sesame oil
2/3 cup white sugar
4 tablespoons garlic, minced
2 tablespoons grated fresh ginger
1 teaspoon freshly ground black pepper

Directions:

Combine all of the sauce ingredients in a pan, and simmer for 10 minutes. Remove from heat, and allow to cool. Set sauce aside.

If the chicken, pork or beef is thick, pound it to thin it out. It will be easier to grill if it's uniform in thickness also. Cut meat into small portion sizes for grilling. Sometimes there are small pieces that won't grill well, so you can soak some wooden skewers in water and use those for the small pieces. Marinate the meat in about 1/2 cup of the sauce for a few hours in the fridge, turning frequently to fully coat.

When it's time, prepare the grill to very hot- around 500 degrees (F). Put 1/2 cup of the sauce in a small dish, and use that to baste onto the meat when grilling.

Put the rest of the sauce in a pan and reheat. Let simmer for about 10 minutes to thicken a little. Once the grill is ready, grill meat on very hot heat to get grill marks on both sides and until the meat is cooked to the desired doneness. At this high heat, it won't take long, so you've got to watch it closely. Paint sauce on both sides while grilling.

Serve with cooked rice and the extra sauce that has been thickened. We like to also serve with Teriyaki Restaurant Style Salad or Asian Coleslaw (see recipes).

Singapore Chili Crab or Shrimp

Serves 4

Ingredients:

2 whole cooked Dungeness crabs
-or- 2 1/2 pounds raw prawns, shelled
1/4 cup tomato ketchup
1 tablespoon hot chili paste
2 tablespoons oyster sauce
1 tablespoon low-sodium soy sauce
1 tablespoon tamarind paste

2 tablespoons peanut oil or avocado oil
2 tablespoons grated fresh ginger
1 1/2 to 2 tablespoons finely chopped garlic
1/2 jalapeño pepper, chopped
2 green onions, chopped thin
2 tablespoons chopped fresh cilantro leaves
more cilantro for garnish

Directions:

For crab, pull the main shell off and discard it. Remove the gray gills and the soft insides. Cut the body in half, and then cut or pull between each leg. Crack the legs and claws with a knife or nut crackers and set aside. If using prawns, peel and de-vein the prawns and set aside.

In a bowl mix the ketchup, chili paste, oyster sauce, soy sauce, and tamarind paste; thin it with 1/4 cup water. Use a stick blender to get tamarind paste a smoother texture and set aside. Pour the oil into a wok or large skillet over med-high heat. Add the green onion, ginger, garlic, jalapeño, and cilantro, and cook for 1 minute. Add the crab or shrimp and stir-fry for another minute. Pour in the sauce and continue cooking, stirring often, until the crab has absorbed the sauce, or the shrimp are fully cooked, and the sauce has thickened, about 5 minutes. If the sauce seems too thick, add a little water.

Serve on top of cooked rice, and garnish with cilantro.

You could also make the sauce ahead, and cook the shrimp ahead, and just add the heated sauce to the shrimp for a quick, no-mess, delicious meal !

Thai Sweet and Sour Pork or Chicken

This turns out just like our favorite Thai restaurant Sweet and Sour. Serve with Rice (or don't!) This recipe ends up being about 3 stars level of spicy. Adjust the chili garlic sauce level to your liking. Instead of sugar, a substitute such as Xylitol can be used. Serves 2

Ingredients:

Sauce:
- 1/3 cup sugar
- 1/3 cup tomato ketchup
- 2 tablespoons chili garlic sauce
- 1/2 cup white rice vinegar
- 1/2 cup water
- 1 teaspoon fish sauce
- corn starch or arrowroot powder

Meat:
- 12 ounces chicken or pork
- 1 tablespoon low-sodium soy sauce
- oil for stir frying- avocado or peanut

Stir Fry Vegetables:
- 1/2 red pepper cut into large pieces
- 1/2 to 1 carrot thinly sliced
- 1/2 to 1 rib celery thinly sliced
- 1/4 yellow onion, cut into 1" pieces
- 1/2 pound asparagus, cut into pieces
- fresh pineapple pieces (optional)
- 2-4 tablespoons finely chopped ginger
- 2-4 tablespoons finely minced garlic

Directions:

Mix sauce ingredients in a small pan, and simmer until slightly reduced. Add 1/2 teaspoon or less of corn starch or arrowroot powder to thicken the sauce, if desired. Set aside until stir fry is complete.

Slice the meat thin, across the grain. Marinate the meat in the soy sauce, and set stand for about an hour. Heat a large wok over medium heat. Once hot, add oil then wait until it's hot, and add meat. Spread out meat on the bottom and sides of wok and let sear for about 1 minute. Stir-fry until cooked through. Remove the meat, and place in a dish.

Let the wok heat up again, and then add another tablespoon of oil. Stir fry peppers, carrots, celery, asparagus, onions until not quite done. Add the garlic and ginger, and stir fry for about another minute. At the very end; throw in the pineapple and meat. Add the sweet and sour sauce into the wok, and stir fry until the pineapple and meat are heated through. The vegetables should be crunchy, not cooked through. Ready to serve!

We sometimes use bean sprouts, snow peas, or green onions cut in 1" pieces instead of yellow onion. You can just use what we've got on hand. The possibilities are endless! We like to make extra sauce and freeze it in portion sizes, it makes stir fry night even faster!

Thai Sweet and Sour Fish

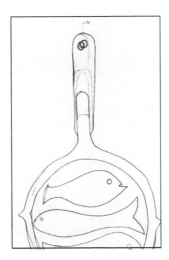

Instead of using pork or chicken, this requires (2) 1/2-inch thick fish fillet pieces. Any white fish can be used for this recipe. We have used black cod fillets, which are wonderful for this dish.

Marinade:
   2 tablespoons rice wine
   2 tablespoons low-sodium soy sauce
   oil for frying- avocado or peanut

Mix together the marinade ingredients. Add the fish and marinate for about an hour. Heat oil in a large wok to medium. Pat the fish dry, and then add it when the oil is hot, turning once, until cooked through. Remove the fish, drain any excess oil, and place on the serving platter. Do not overcook the fish, it will continue cooking a bit when the sauce is put on it.

Use the same sauce, vegetables, and directions for stir frying as the Thai Sweet and Sour Pork or Chicken recipe.

Korean BBQ Kalbi Beef Ribs

Serves 4

Ingredients:

3-4 pounds flanken-style ribs
marinade

Marinade:

1/2 cup soy sauce
1 Asian pear, grated with juices
2 tablespoons garlic, grated
1/2 small white onion, grated
1 tablespoon fresh ginger, grated
1/4 cup dark brown sugar
1/2 tablespoon honey
2 tablespoons sesame seeds, toasted
2 tablespoons toasted sesame oil
1/4 teaspoon ground black pepper
1 tablespoon Korean ground red pepper (Gochugaru)
2 green onions, chopped

Directions:

Grate garlic, onion, ginger, and pear. Mix all ingredients in a gallon zip bag. Add meat and marinate overnight.

Prepare grill to very hot- around 500 degrees (F). Shake and rub off excess marinade. Grill on a very hot grill to desired doneness, recommend done medium to medium rare.

Serve with:
Cooked rice
Prepared Korean kimchee.
Pajeon or Korean green onion pancake with dipping sauce
Teriyaki Restaurant Style Salad, or Asian Coleslaw (see recipes)

Greek

Dolmathes- Lamb Stuffed Grape Leaves
(Also called Yaprikia in Greece)

Ingredients:

1 pound ground lamb
1 medium yellow onion, diced
1 cup raw rice
3 tablespoons extra virgin olive oil
2 tablespoons dried mint
beef stock or broth
1 jar grape leaves (about 25-40 leaves)
1/4 teaspoon freshly ground pepper

Directions:

We use either ground lamb or leg of lamb, and then grind our own. 15-20% fat works best for this.

Combine meat, rice, onion, mint, 3 tablespoons olive oil, and a little pepper. Remove the grape leaves from the jar and shake off any excess fluid. Don't rinse grape leaves, a little brine with the leaves adds flavor. Lay out grape leaves with shiny side down (veins up) and the stem of the leaves towards you. Place about 1 1/2 to 2 heaping tablespoon filling in the center of a grape leaf. The amount should fit the size of the leaf. Roll up; tucking sides in. It should look rather like a short fat cigar. Continue rolling until all filling is used up; around 25 dolmathes (give or take).

To cook, coat the bottom of sauce pan with olive oil. Arrange the dolmathes side by side, close together in a pan, making more than one layer if necessary. Pour about 2 tablespoons olive oil over the top. If using homemade beef stock, be sure it has been seasoned with salt. Pour enough beef stock over to barely cover the dolmathes. Cover with a heavy heat-proof plate. This is important, if you skip the plate, the dolmathes tend to fall apart. Cover sauce pan; bring to boil; lower heat, and simmer for about 45 minutes. Check one to make sure the rice is cooked.

May be served warm or at room temperature. Serve with Egg and Lemon Sauce (see recipe), or with just lemon wedges.

Note: Dolmathes can be frozen after they are cooked. Just lay them out individually and put in the freezer, and then once frozen, put them into a plastic zip bag. You could also freeze in portion sizes in multiple packages. Thaw them fully before heating to serve. Even the Egg and Lemon Sauce freezes nicely.

Egg and Lemon Sauce (Avgolemono Sauce)

3 eggs- room temperature
4 tablespoons juice of fresh lemon, or to taste
1 teaspoon cornstarch dissolved in a little water
1/2 cup Greek yogurt
1 cup left over dolmathes liquid- slightly cooled

Directions:

Add eggs to a jar with a lid, and shake well. Add corn starch mix and lemon juice, and shake again. Add yogurt, and shake again. Set aside until the dolmathes are done. Pour the egg mixture into a small sauce pan. Add the 1 cup of hot broth, and turn stove on to medium-low. Stir frequently to start, and when it starts to thicken, stir constantly. Taste to see if it's lemony enough for your taste, and add a little more if desired. Continue to stir constantly until thickened, it just takes a few minutes.

Canned Grape Leaves

We have a grape vine in our yard, so we can our own grape leaves. It's so incredibly simple.

Ingredients:

3 jars with sealable lids- sterilized
1 quart water
1/2 cup juice from fresh lemon
1/4 cup salt
72 fresh grape leaves
kitchen string

Directions:

Bring water to a boil, add salt and dissolve. Add lemon juice. Meanwhile wash the leaves, and snip off the stems. Stack the leaves in 12 leaves per bunch. Roll tightly and tie with kitchen string. Add the bundles to the boiling water, and blanch for 2 minutes until they change color and soften. Remove from water, and pack into jars of 2 bundles per jar.

Bring water back to a rolling boil. Pour the boiling water into the jars, leaving about 1/4 inch of space. Use a clean chop stick to be sure any air bubbles get out. Immediately put the lids on and tighten. Let them sit on the counter to fully cool without touching them. They should seal, and then you can put them in the pantry for up to a year. Any jar that does not seal, should be refrigerated and just use that one first.

As always with home canned goods, never use the jar if the color, odor, or texture is not right. Also, if it's cloudy or not sealed when you open it, toss it out.

Grilled Lamb Chops

Lamb chops go great as part of a Greek meal. Serve this Greek feast with Retsina (a traditional Greek white wine), and you feel like you're on Paros!   Serves 4

Ingredients:

5-6 lamb chops, 1-2 per person, depending on thickness

Marinade:

2 tablespoons juice from lemon
2 tablespoons good extra virgin olive oil
1/2 teaspoon dried oregano
1/4 teaspoon salt
1/4 teaspoon freshly ground black pepper

Directions:

Combine marinade ingredients, and add to a gallon zip bag. Add chops, shake, and marinate for about 2 or 3 hours, turning to coat all over.

Prepare your grill by cleaning and reheating to very hot, about 500-550 degrees (F). Once the grill is ready and the rest of dinner is within 15 minutes, begin to grill by placing chops on their fat cap first. You have to watch them because they can flame and/or fall over. You can only do this with thick chops. Otherwise, grill the chops like you would steak to your desired amount of doneness. Lamb tends to cook fairly quickly as compared to other cuts of meat.

After they come off the grill, place the plate on a hot pad (to help keep them warm) and cover with foil. Let rest about 5 to 7 minutes.

Lamb Souvlaki

These Greek grilled lamb kabobs are one of our family's favorites to have with a Greek meal. You can eat them served with hummus and tzatziki, or you can serve them in a pita like a gyro. We typically use leg of lamb for this. Along with the lamb, sometimes we like to grill mushrooms, onions, and/or red peppers.

Ingredients:

2 pounds lamb, cut into 1 1/2 inch cubes
1/2 cup freshly squeezed lemon juice
1/2 cup extra virgin olive oil
1 1/2 tablespoons dried oregano
1/2 teaspoon salt
freshly ground pepper to taste

Directions:

Mix the marinade ingredients together. Place the pieces of meat in a gallon zip bag or a non-reactive dish. Pour the marinade over the meat, making sure it's fully coated. Let marinate in the fridge for 6-8 hours, turning occasionally.

Make skewers with the meat. You can add veggies to the skewers as well, as desired. If using wooden skewers, soak the skewers for 30 minutes before using to prevent them from burning.

Prepare grill and heat to very hot. Grill to desired doneness. We like ours cooked to about medium rare. Let rest covered for 5 minutes before serving.

Chicken Souvlaki

Serves 4

Ingredients:

1 1/2 pounds boneless skinless chicken breasts or thighs
1 tablespoon Greek Seasoning (see recipe)
salt to taste
1 teaspoon dried oregano
2 teaspoons juice from lemon
2 tablespoons extra-virgin olive oil

Directions:

Mix all of the ingredients except the chicken and set aside. Cut the chicken into pieces to put on skewers or in strips as desired. Marinate the chicken for about 1 hour before skewering. If using wooden skewers soak them in water for 20 minutes before using.

Prepare a grill to very hot. Just before placing the chicken on the grill, oil the grill. Grill the chicken on all sides until cooked through and you have nice grill marks. Let sit 5 minutes covered with foil before serving.

This is nice served with Tzatziki (see recipe).

Mediterranean Chicken with Artichokes

Serves 4

Ingredients:

2 chicken breasts, skinless and boneless
6 ounces marinated artichoke hearts, cut bite-sized
3 cups chicken stock or broth
1/8 teaspoon red pepper flakes
salt and freshly ground pepper to taste
1 teaspoon cornstarch in a little water
1 tablespoon juice from a lemon
1/2 teaspoon dill leaves
1 tablespoon capers
Greek olives cut into quarters
flour for dredging
extra virgin olive oil for frying
1 tablespoon butter
crumbled feta cheese

Directions:

Cut chicken breasts horizontally, and then pound chicken to get even thickness. Salt and pepper the chicken. Dredge them in the flour, and fry chicken pieces in the olive oil until just cooked through. Remove chicken to a plate, and add broth, pepper flakes, salt, and pepper to the pan. Simmer 5 minutes to slightly reduce. Add dill, lemon juice, and cornstarch, and cook until thickened. Add chicken and heat. Add artichokes, capers, and olives, and bring back to a boil. Stir in butter at the very end.

Serve chicken with sauce and crumbled feta as a garnish over the top.

Serve with Greek Lemon Rice (see recipe)

Braised Chicken with Artichokes and Olives

The taste of this is a bit similar to a tapenade. You are going to want to spoon some of the drippings over rice. If you prefer a sauce that's a little thickened, just add 1 tablespoon of flour to the liquids before baking. Serves 2-4

Ingredients:

2 or 4 chicken thighs, bone in with skin
extra virgin olive oil
4 garlic cloves
2 or 3 large artichokes
1/4 cup each Kalamata and green olives
1/2 cup water from artichoke
1/2 cup chicken stock or broth
1 teaspoon each thyme and oregano
2 teaspoons capers
2 teaspoons juice from lemon
salt and freshly ground pepper
2 tablespoons butter

Directions:

Prepare artichokes ahead of time: Pluck off any small leaves on the outside and discard. Cut off the very tops of the artichokes using a large knife. Snip off the sharp ends from the remaining leaves using kitchen scissors. Trim the ends of the stems. Use a peeler and peel the outside off of the stems. Wash and put in a large pot and add 1-2 inches of water. Steam covered for about 45-50 minutes (for large artichokes), or until they are soft and a fork is easily inserted into the heart. Drain and let cool, reserving 1/2 cup of the cooking water.

Once cool enough to handle, remove the outer leaves leaving just the heart. Cut the heart into quarters and set aside along with the stem. The leaves can be used for a side dish or tomorrow's lunch. Pit and halve the olives.

Pat chicken dry using paper towels. Season the skin with salt. Using a fry pan, fry the chicken on medium heat, skin side down, in olive oil until the skin is dark golden brown, around 15 minutes. When the skin is browned, season the bottom side of the chicken with salt, pepper, oregano, and thyme. Transfer the chicken to the baking pan, and place skin side up. Add the frying pan drippings to the baking pan. Also add the garlic cloves, olives, capers, artichoke cooking water, lemon, and chicken broth to the pan. Bake uncovered at 350 degrees (F).

After 30 minutes of baking, add the artichoke hearts and butter to the pan, and stir in just a little bit. Continue cooking until the chicken is done, and the artichokes are heated through.

125

Indian

Chicken Tikka Masala

Spice mixture: Mix all ingredients together
- 6 garlic cloves, finely grated
- 4 teaspoons ginger, finely grated
- 1 1/2 tablespoons curry powder
- 1 teaspoon ground coriander
- 1/2 teaspoons ground cumin
- 1 1/2 teaspoons chili powder
- 1 teaspoon ground cardamom

Meat Marinade: Refrigerate 4-6 hours.
- 1/2 of spice mixture
- 1 cup Greek yogurt
- 2 pounds chicken breasts, cut bite size

Sauce:
- 3 tablespoons olive oil
- 3 tablespoons salted butter
- 1 small yellow onion, thinly sliced
- 1-2 serrano chilis or large jalapeños, chopped
- 1 28-ounce can whole peeled tomatoes
- 1 1/2 cups heavy cream or half and half
- 3/4 cup chopped fresh cilantro
- 1/4 cup tomato paste (2 ounces)

Directions:

Sauté onion and chilies in olive oil in a large pot over medium heat, stirring often until caramelized. Add remaining 1/2 of spice mixture, butter, and tomato paste, and cook, stirring often, until bottom of pot begins to brown, about 4 minutes. Add tomatoes with juices, crushing them with your hands. Bring to a boil, reduce heat, and simmer, stirring often until sauce thickens, 10-15 minutes.

Preheat broiler. Arrange marinated chicken on a foil-lined rimmed baking sheet in a single layer. Broil on the top rack until chicken starts to blacken in spots (it will not be cooked through), about 8- 10 minutes.

Meanwhile, add cream, leftover marinade, and chopped cilantro to the sauce. At this point, use a stick blender to make the sauce smooth (optional). Simmer, stirring occasionally until sauce thickens, about 10-15 minutes. Add chicken pieces to the sauce, and stir occasionally until chicken is cooked through, 8-10 minutes. Taste and add salt if needed. Serve with steamed rice. Raita goes well with this dish (see recipe).

Chicken Curry

This is a nice (and spicy!) one pot meal. We like to add cauliflower, carrots, asparagus, mushrooms, or broccoli (whatever we have on hand) in at the last 15-20 minutes of cooking. Raita (see recipe) goes well with this dish as a 'cooling' side. Serves 4

Ingredients:

1 chicken cut into pieces bone-in
3 tablespoons olive oil
1 1/2 large onion, chopped
5 garlic cloves, minced or grated
1" peeled ginger, minced or grated
1 tablespoon hot curry powder
2 tablespoons regular curry powder

1 1/2 teaspoons ground coriander
1/2 teaspoon ground cumin
1/4 teaspoon cayenne (or to taste)
1 teaspoon chili power
1 28-ounce can peeled tomatoes
vegetables cut into bite size pieces
chicken stock or broth (optional)

Directions:

Heat olive oil in a large heavy pot over medium heat. Brown the chicken pieces skin side down. You can skip this step if using skinless chicken. Once brown, move to a separate dish and set aside. Add more oil to the pot if needed, and add onion. Sauté over medium heat until quite brown (important). Add the ginger and garlic, and fry one minute. Add the coriander powder, and fry one minute. Add the remaining spices, and fry 30 seconds. Add 1 cup water, and simmer 5 minutes.

Add tomatoes with juices, crushing them with your hands as you add them. Bring to a boil, reduce heat, and simmer, stirring often and scraping up browned bits from bottom of pot, until sauce thickens, about 10 minutes.

Put the chicken in the pot with enough water (or chicken stock) to cover, and simmer covered until tender, approximately 1 1/4 hours. Put any vegetables that you are using in during the last 15-30 minutes of cooking, depending on what veggies you use. Remove the chicken from the curry, and once it's cool enough to handle, bone it and return to the pot. Taste and add salt if needed. Serve with steamed rice.

Quick Beef or Chicken Curry

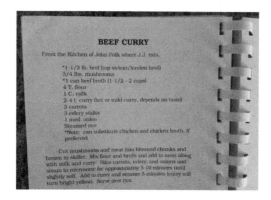

This is the recipe that John used to make curry when he had to get dinner on the table quickly after work when our kids were young. Everyone really loved it ! It got put into a Brier Elementary Recipe book in 1994 that was a collection of recipes from the families at the school. Serves 4

Ingredients:

1 1/2 pounds top sirloin beef (or chicken)

3/4 pound mushrooms

1 1/2 to 2 cups beef stock or broth (or chicken)

4 tablespoons flour

1 cup milk

2-4 teaspoons curry powder (hot or mild or mix, to taste)

3 med carrots

3 celery ribs

1 med yellow onion

salt and freshly ground pepper to taste

Directions:

Cut mushrooms and meat into bite-sized pieces, and brown in a skillet. Mix flour and stock together, and add to the meat along with the milk, curry powder, salt, and pepper. Slice carrots, celery, and onions, and steam in the microwave for about 5-10 minutes until slightly soft. Add to curry, and simmer 5 minutes. Serve over steamed rice.

Keema

Serves 4

Ingredients:

1 pound ground beef
1 cup chopped onion
1 tablespoon minced fresh ginger
1 1/2 teaspoons hot curry powder
2 teaspoons regular curry powder
1/2 teaspoon cardamom powder
1 teaspoon minced garlic
2 tablespoons minced jalapeño pepper
1/2 teaspoon salt
1/4 teaspoon ground pepper
1/2 cup chicken stock or broth
1 cup canned tomatoes, diced
-or- 2 med seeded fresh tomatoes, diced
3/4 cup frozen peas
cooked rice

Directions:

Heat pan with oil and add onions. Cook onions until caramelized. Remove onions from pan and set aside. Add ground beef to the pan and cook through. Remove any excess fat from pan, and then add onions back to pan. If using a low-fat content beef, you do not need to remove the onions from the pan before cooking the beef.

Add rest of the ingredients except peas, and simmer until the garlic, ginger, and jalapeño are cooked through. At the end add the peas, and cook just until the peas are done.

Serve over rice.

Italian

Meatballs

Use meatballs for spaghetti or for meatball subs. We eat them just plain with sauce and Parmesan cheese also! Makes about 14 meatballs.

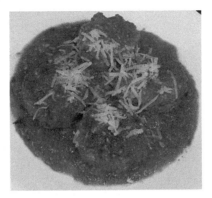

Ingredients:

1 pound ground beef
1/2 cup bread crumbs (or can use oatmeal)
1/3 cup Parmesan cheese
grated Parmesan cheese for serving
1 egg

1/3 cup finely chopped fresh parsley
1/2 teaspoon dried oregano
1 clove minced garlic
oil for frying (if needed)
Marinara sauce, or Arrabiata Sauce (see recipes)

Directions:

If using oatmeal instead of bread crumbs, put the oats into a food processor, and pulse a few times to make them finer. Mix all of the ingredients in a bowl. If using low fat content ground beef, add oil to a pan for frying. Oil may not be needed to fry meat with a higher fat content. Shape the meatballs into balls about 1 1/2 to 2 inches in diameter, and place in a frying pan. Fry and turn them until the meatballs are nice and brown all over.

Add sauce to the pan, and continue to cook the meat and sauce until the meatballs are done all the way through, about 10 minutes. Serve with cooked pasta if desired. Sprinkle freshly grated Parmesan over the top and serve!

For meatball subs, put on a French roll and top with mozzarella or provolone cheese. Broil until the cheese is melted and the bread starting to brown. Delicious!

Lasagna

Serves 4-5   Makes an 8x9x3" pan

Ingredients:

- 1 pound lean ground beef
- 2 cups Marinara + extra for serving (see recipe)
- 8 ounces mozzarella cheese
- 1/2 cup grated Parmesan cheese
- 1/4 large yellow onion, diced
- 1 cup mushrooms, sliced
- 1/2 pound lasagna pasta
- 12 ounces ricotta cheese
    - (for Fresh Ricotta Cheese, see recipe)

Directions:

Using a large pot, sauté the onions until soft. Add the beef and mushrooms. Sauté until the meat is just cooked. Add the 2 cups of marinara, and simmer until heated through.

Make Homemade Fresh Pasta (see recipe), or cook the lasagna per the directions on the package if using. Leave the pasta very al dente since it will cook more while baking. Drain and set aside.

Ladle a little meat sauce into the bottom of a baking dish. Put a layer of pasta, then a little more sauce. Add a layer of ricotta and Parmesan cheese. Add another layer of sauce and pasta. Add more sauce and mozzarella cheese. Add a little more sauce and another layer of pasta. Continue layering until all except a little sauce, mozzarella, and some Parmesan are used up. How to layer is completely free form.

Finish by putting the remaining sauce and Parmesan cheese on top. Do not put the remaining mozzarella cheese on yet. Bake in a 350 degree (F) oven for about 45 minutes until bubbling inside, adding the mozzarella cheese during the last 15 minutes. Let rest for about 10 minutes before serving. Cut into squares and serve, ladling a little marinara on top of each piece.

A low carb version of this includes using artichoke hearts or sliced portobello mushrooms instead of pasta. If using portobellos, sauté the mushrooms first to release their juices before using in the lasagna.

Also, lasagna can easily be frozen in portion sizes for quick and easy (and tasty!) dinners when desired. One way is to cook the whole lasagna in a large baking pan, and when fully cooled, refrigerate it. It can then be cut into portion size squares and each wrapped in plastic wrap and then several portions put into a large zip bag. You can grab one or two portions that way. Fully thaw and transfer to a baking pan. Cover with foil and bake at 300 degrees (F) to heat. Also, you could freeze any extra marinara to go along with your frozen lasagna.

Fresh Pasta

Ingredients:

2 cups flour, plus more for the work surface
1/2 teaspoon salt
3 extra-large or jumbo eggs
water if needed

Directions:

This simple recipe is made even simpler if you make the pasta in the morning if you are using it for dinner. If pasta with more "chew" is desired, you can use 1 cup flour and 1 cup semolina.

Put the flour and salt in a food processor bowl. Whir it a bit to mix. Drop all of the eggs in at once. Process the dough until a ball forms (10 seconds or less). If it seems too dry, add a teaspoon of water. If it seems too wet, add a tablespoon more flour. Once the ball has formed, continue processing for 30 seconds more. Pour the dough onto your work surface, using a little flour to keep it from sticking. Form it into a ball with your hands, working it just a bit if it seems like it wants to fall apart. Wrap the ball tightly with plastic wrap, and set on the counter in a cool dark place until ready to use in the afternoon. This will help the glutens form. By using this method, no kneading is required!

When the pasta has rested on the counter for most of the day, cut it in pieces for rolling. Flour your work surface, and use a rolling pin to get the pasta quite thin. Another other option is to use pasta machine. Begin rolling the pasta at the thickest setting, and each time reduce the thickness until you get to the desired thickness. Remember, it puffs up when you cook it.

Note: Fresh pasta requires significantly less time to cook. Lasagna sheets can cook in as little as 1-2 minutes since it will also be baking in the sauce. Homemade pasta makes some dishes all that much better! Makes about 1 pound of pasta

Ravioli

Ravioli is a big subject- you can make many different fillings, and use many different sauces. We've seen deep-fried ravioli in restaurants even! Here are some fillings that we have used:

Ingredients:

ravioli filling
Fresh Pasta (see recipe)
1 egg, lightly beaten
lots of flour for the work surface

Fresh Herb and Cheese Ravioli – mix together 1 15-ounce container of ricotta cheese and 1/2 cup grated Parmesan cheese, plus desired amount of fresh oregano, thyme, and parley. Add 1 lightly beaten egg and pepper.

Spinach and Cheese Ravioli- mix together 1 10-ounce package of frozen chopped spinach, about 1 cup ricotta cheese, salt and pepper to taste, 2 tablespoons half and half, 1 egg, 4 tablespoons Parmesan cheese, and 1 1/2 tablespoons chopped fresh parsley.

Beef Ravioli- Mix together 1/2 pound ground beef, 1 clove garlic, pressed, 2 tablespoons grated Parmesan cheese, 2 tablespoons bread crumbs, and 1 1/2 tablespoons chopped fresh parsley. Add 1 lightly beaten egg.

Directions:

Note: The pasta should be made in the morning for use in the afternoon. Make the filling and set aside. Lightly beat the egg and set aside.

Roll the pasta into very thin (#5 setting on the roller), 4-inch wide sheets. Do keep in mind that when the pasta is cooked, it will double in thickness. While making the ravioli, keep the pasta sheets covered with a damp towel to prevent them from drying out. Also be sure your work surface has plenty of flour- the pasta is quite sticky. Extra flour on the ravioli is OK; you can dust off the excess and then any left-over just comes off in the water when you boil them.

Put 1-2 teaspoons of filling in piles, about 3 inches apart, in a line on 1/2 of the pasta lengthwise. Paint in between the filling piles and around all 4 edges with beaten egg. Fold the pasta in half lengthwise, over the filling. Pat the pasta down over the filling, trying to get out as much air as you can.

Use a knife to cut in between the ravioli to separate them. Use a fork to crimp the cut sides of each one. Place ravioli in a single layer on wax paper until ready to cook, making sure the bottom is dusted with flour to prevent sticking. If the pasta will be sitting a significant amount of time before cooking, cover with plastic wrap.

Cook ravioli in boiling water for 3-5 minutes, or until the pasta is cooked how you like it. Fresh pasta will not take as long as dried pasta.

If you will be using sauce with the Ravioli, heat the sauce before cooking the ravioli. Add a little hot sauce to the bottom of a serving dish. Once the ravioli are done, put them in the dish. You may want to add sauce on top before layering more ravioli on top of the first ones to prevent them from sticking together. If not using sauce, you can just put a little olive oil on the plate to prevent sticking.

Ravioli can be frozen after they are made, and before they are cooked. Just lay them out in a single layer on a cookie sheet lined with wax paper. Cover with plastic wrap and put the tray in the freezer. Once frozen, remove from tray and place in a plastic zip bag, and remove as much air as possible. Return the bag to the freezer for a quick and delicious dinner in the near future!

Chicago Italian Beef Sandwiches
with Spicy Giardiniera

We sometimes go to a sandwich shop in Arizona called *Luke's*. This is where we first had a great Italian beef sandwich. We've since had them in other Chicago Deli type restaurants. The key to making the best sandwich is finding good Chicago-style giardiniera. It can be hard to find, so we actually bought ours on line! These sandwiches are as spicy as you like. The giardiniera we get is quite spicy, and the roasted poblanos can add heat as well. Messy and delicious! Serves 4

Ingredients:

2 pounds top round roast or similar
1 stick of French bread or hard rolls
4-8 slices provolone cheese
spicy giardiniera
2 cups beef broth
1 teaspoon thyme
2 roasted poblano peppers (optional)

Directions:

Freeze the meat until about 1/2 frozen. Use a slicer or a knife to slice very thin, across the grain. Refrigerate until time to use. Roast, skin, seed, and slice poblano peppers if using. Set aside.

Pour the broth into a saucepan, and add the thyme. Simmer about 10 minutes to blend the flavors. Cut the bread in half lengthwise and to the desired size for your sandwiches. Place bread pieces on a sheet pan with sides, open-faced.

When it is dinner time, bring the broth to a rolling boil. Put the thin-sliced meat into the broth and stir. Heat until the meat is to the desired doneness. It won't take long! Using tongs put the meat onto the bread. Spoon some broth (however much you'd like) onto the meat and bread. Add the giardiniera and poblano slices if using, to the desired amount. Put slices of cheese over the open-faced sandwich.

Broil until the cheese is melted and the bread is brown on the edges. Serve hot. You're going to need a lot of napkins!

Spicy Italian Sausage

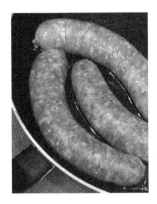

If you prefer non-spicy, just leave out the red pepper flakes and cayenne pepper. This sausage is just great used in Spaghetti or Meatballs, as well as Sausage and Peppers Sandwiches (see recipe). We make it as both ground sausage and sausages stuffed into hog casings to freeze. The cased sausages are great pan fried or grilled.

Ingredients:

- 4 pounds pork butt or pork shoulder (with fat)
- 1 tablespoon fennel seeds
- 1 tablespoon fresh finely minced garlic
- 1 tablespoon red pepper flakes
- 4 teaspoons kosher salt
- 2 teaspoons freshly ground black pepper
- 1 teaspoon cayenne pepper

Directions:

Cut the pork into small enough cubes to fit into a meat grinder. Use a meat grinder to grind to medium grind- not too fine. Put ground meat into a large bowl. Add the seasonings to the bowl and mix with your hands until fully mixed. Cover and refrigerate overnight for the best result, to help the flavors blend.

Package into portion sized freezer zip bags, or stuff into casings and freeze in portion sizes.

Sausage and Pepper Sandwiches

Ingredients:

Italian sausages- 1 per person
hard rolls, such as balillo rolls- 1 per person
1 red pepper
1-2 fresh poblano peppers

1 yellow onion
1-2 cups marinara sauce
sliced provolone or mozzarella cheese
extra virgin olive oil for frying

Directions:

Cut the onions and peppers into strips. Fry the poblano peppers on medium-high heat for 5 minutes, then add the rest of the peppers and onions. Continue to fry until they are a bit browned and soft, but not mushy. The poblanos take a little longer than red peppers and onions. Remove from heat and set aside.

Add 2 tablespoons olive oil to a frying pan. Add the sausages. Add water to the pan until the sausages are in about 1/8 inch water. Fry them on medium heat until they are cooked through, turning once. By the time they are cooked, the water should be evaporated. If the water has evaporated before they are cooked, just add a little more as needed. Once they are cooked through, just brown them on both sides and remove from heat.

Heat up the marinara. Slice the rolls or bread, and layer it with sausage, peppers, and cheese. Broil on high to melt the cheese and get some browning on the bread. Remove from broiler and ladle hot marinara on top. Serve immediately with lots of napkins!

Chicken Piccata

Serves 4

Ingredients:

2 large skinless and boneless chicken breasts
salt and freshly ground black pepper
flour for dredging
8 tablespoons butter
3 tablespoons extra-virgin olive oil for frying
3 tablespoons fresh lemon juice
2 cups chicken stock or broth
3 tablespoons brined capers
1 tablespoon fresh parsley, chopped
up to 1 tablespoon corn starch or arrowroot, if needed to thicken

Directions:

Butterfly chicken breasts or just cut to half thickness. Use plastic wrap below and above chicken, and pound chicken very thin (less than 1/4 inch). They will plump up when cooking. Cut into serving size pieces. Pat the chicken pieces dry with a paper towel. Season with salt and pepper as desired (we use salted butter, so we do not add salt at this stage). Dredge the chicken in flour, and shake off excess.

In a large skillet over medium high heat, melt 2 tablespoons of butter with 3 tablespoons olive oil. When butter and oil is hot, add the chicken pieces and cook for 3 minutes. When chicken is browned, flip and cook other side for 3 minutes. Remove and transfer to plate.

Add the lemon juice, stock, and capers to the pan. Bring to boil, scraping up brown bits from the bottom of the pan. Simmer until slightly reduced. Add remaining butter to the pan. Add corn starch or arrowroot if needed, and stir until slightly thickened. Return the chicken to the pan, and simmer until heated through. Garnish with parsley and serve.

Chicken or Veal Parmesan

Serves 4

Ingredients:

2 large chicken breasts or 1 to 1 1/2 pounds veal
1/2 cup panko crumbs
1/2 cup grated Parmesan cheese
1/2 cup flour for dredging
2 eggs
1/2 cup grated mozzarella cheese
1/2 cup grated Fontina cheese
marinara sauce

Directions:

Prepare chicken breasts: If the breasts are thick, cut them to half thickness. Pound them flat to make uniform in thickness- about 1/4 inch thick.

Put lightly beaten egg in a dish. In another dish, add the flour and pepper to taste. Combine crumbs and Parmesan in a third separate dish. Dip meat pieces first into the flour mixture, and shake off excess. Dip into the egg, and then dip in crumbs/ Parmesan mixture, and shake off excess. Set coated pieces on a plate.

Heat oil in a frying pan until the oil is quite hot. Fry the chicken or veal on both sides quite hot and quick, until golden brown and cooked through. Move pieces to a cookie sheet. Mix grated cheeses, and put 1/4 cup on top of each piece of cooked chicken. Broil until cheese is fully melted. Alternately, after the chicken is about done, leave in the frying pan, put cheese on top, then cover with lid or foil, and cook to let the cheese melt (making this a one-pan meal!)

Serve with marinara on top of chicken or veal pieces. Serve with your favorite pasta if desired, and a fresh Italian salad.

Veal Marsala

Serves 4

Ingredients:

8 pieces of veal scaloppini, or cutlet- pounded thin
1 small shallot, finely chopped
3 cloves garlic, finely chopped
8 ounces mushrooms, quartered
1/2 cup Marsala wine
1/3 cup dry red wine
2 tablespoons butter
1/2 teaspoon dried thyme
1 cup chicken stock or broth
1/4 cup extra-virgin olive oil
1/2 cup flour
salt and freshly ground black pepper
2 tablespoons half and half
chopped fresh parsley for garnish

Directions:

In a non-stick frying pan, heat the olive oil over medium high heat. Season the flour with salt and pepper. Dredge the veal in the flour, and shake off excess. Add them to the pan and fry until just golden on both sides, and remove them from the pan. This will not take long since they are very thin.

Add more olive oil to the pan if needed and heat. Sauté the shallots, garlic, and mushrooms, until they are mostly cooked through. Add the thyme, Marsala, red wine, and broth. Bring to a boil, and reduce by one third. Add the butter, and replace the veal in the pan. Bring just to a boil, reduce the heat, and simmer for 5 to 6 minutes to heat through.

Taste the sauce and add salt and pepper as needed. Transfer the veal to a platter, and pour the sauce over the meat. Serve with egg noodles or orzo.

Cioppino

Serves 4

Ingredients:

1 large live Dungeness crab, or cooked- with shells
2 pounds live clams
1/2 pound raw prawns
1/2 pound raw scallops
1/2 pound fish fillets (cod, halibut, etc.), cut into large cubes
1 28-ounce can Italian tomatoes
1 8-ounce can tomato sauce
4 cups seafood stock (see recipe below)
2 16-ounce cans clam nectar
1/2 cups dry white wine
1/4 cup extra virgin olive oil
2 cups chopped yellow onion
3 tablespoons finely chopped garlic
3 tablespoons finely chopped fresh basil leaves
3 tablespoons chopped parsley
1 teaspoon chopped fresh oregano leaves
1 teaspoon chopped fresh thyme leaves
1 teaspoon freshly ground black pepper
salt to taste
1 teaspoon red pepper flakes, optional

Directions:

If using a live Dungeness crab, use a large heavy knife and quickly stab the underside of the crab in the middle between the eyes, and cut down between the leg clusters. The crab will separate at this point. Discard the feathers and the green liquid. Save the body shells. Separate the leg sections and set aside. Peel and de-vein the prawns, saving the shells. Set the raw shrimp aside.

In a large pot, add all of the prawn and crab shells. Fill with water to cover (about 5 cups) and boil for about 20 minutes. Strain out the liquid and discard the shells. Set aside stock.

In a large stock pot over high heat, add oil, and slowly cook onions and garlic until soft and translucent, about 10 minutes. Add the basil, 1/2 of the parsley, oregano, thyme, and black pepper. Add red pepper flakes, if using. Add canned tomatoes, tomato sauce, seafood stock, clam nectar, and wine, and bring to a boil. Reduce heat to a simmer, and cook about 1 hour for the flavors to blend. Taste, and add salt and freshly ground pepper if needed.

Meanwhile, clean the clams by rinsing them in cold water. For any that are slightly open, if they are still alive, when you tap on them they will close up. Discard any that are not fully closed. Refrigerate until ready to use.

About 15 minutes before serving, start to add seafood. Bring the broth to a rolling boil. Add the crabs as they will take about 15 minutes to cook. About 5 minutes after the crabs are added, add the clams. About 5 minutes later, add the prawns. After 2 minutes, add the scallops and fish fillets and cook for 3 minutes, or until the clams open. Check that all of the seafood is completely cooked. Discard any unopened clams. If using cooked Dungeness crab, add at the end with the fish and scallops.

Serve in individual bowls with a nice rustic bread. Garnish with the other half of the parsley. You'll need crab crackers, a bowl for shells, and plenty of napkins at the table as well.

Homemade Pizza

Teresa likes thin-crust, John likes thicker-crust. Everybody can build their own pizza! Pizza night has always been a lot of fun at our house. Makes 2-3 individual-sized pizzas.

Dough:

- 1 1/2 cups all-purpose flour
- 1 tablespoon (1 package) active dry yeast
- 1/2 cup plus 2 tablespoons cold water
- 1 tablespoon olive oil
- 1/4 teaspoon salt

Directions:

Add water and olive oil to a measuring cup. Set aside.

Add flour, salt and yeast to a food processor bowl. Whir to mix, and then pour in the water/ olive oil mixture. Whir it until it forms a ball, then keep whirring it for an additional 30 seconds. If it seems too wet, add a little more flour. If it doesn't come together in 1 ball, add more water. Pour the dough out onto a floured work surface and knead one or two times, just until it forms a nice smooth ball.

Place into an oiled container, cover, and put into the refrigerator for at least overnight, and up to 3 nights.

When ready to use, flour your work surface. Remove dough from refrigerator and pour the dough out onto the work surface. Very gently shape into 2 large-sized, or 3 medium-sized balls, using flour as needed to prevent sticking. Sprinkle a little flour on the dough on the top of the dough and cover with plastic wrap. Let rest at room temperature for at least 2 hours covered.

Preheat the oven to 550 degrees (F) with a pizza stone in the oven, set in the lower 1/3 of the oven. Allow the stone to heat for 45 minutes to 1 hour before using.

145

Using your hands and just enough flour to prevent sticking, stretch the dough working it as little as possible. Shape from the middle, out, using your fingers, and keeping the edges intact. Transfer the dough to a flat sheet pan or a pizza peel that has been dusted with semolina or corn meal.

Put desired toppings on the crust and then slide the pizza directly onto the heated stone. Bake until the crust and cheese is the desired brownness, about 7 or 8 minutes. Rotate the pizza half way through cooking to get even doneness. If you don't have a pizza stone, baking on a cookie sheet will work, but do not preheat like you do a stone.

One key to a great crust is to cook it as hot as possible so that the crust is brown without the middle of it drying out. If your BBQ gets hotter than 550 degrees (F), another good option is to put the pizza stone in the BBQ and heat it for 1 hour before using. If cooking hotter, the pizza may not take as long.

Pizza Sauce: Simmer in a sauce pan until nice and thick.

1 14-ounce can of tomatoes, pureed or can use sauce
1/3 cup tomato paste, or 1/2 cup paste if using sauce
1/2 teaspoon each oregano and thyme
salt and freshly ground pepper to taste

Some of our favorite pizza toppings: use toppings or make just plain cheese!

blend of mozzarella, Fontina, and Parmesan cheeses
dry salami, or pre-cooked sausage
black olives
pepperoncini slices

mushrooms
artichoke hearts
fresh tomatoes slices after baking
extra Italian herbs

Side Dishes

Popovers

Popovers use the same batter as Yorkshire pudding, also called *Yorkies*. Traditionally, Yorkies are made as a loaf in a pan rather than individual muffins, with the drippings from beef put in the bottom of the pan. Either way- Yum! Makes 10 muffins.

Ingredients:

2 tablespoons melted butter or oil

eggs- 3 jumbo or 4 large, room temperature

1 cup milk, room temperature

beef fat cut into 1/8 to 1/4 inch cubes (optional)

1 cup all-purpose flour

1/2 teaspoon kosher salt

oil for pan- avocado for high heat cooking

Directions:

Mix the eggs and milk. In a separate bowl, mix the flour and salt. Add the egg mixture to the flour mixture, and whisk a little. Add the melted butter or oil, and mix until smooth. Do not over-mix. Do not mix the wet and dry ingredients until time to bake.

Preheat the oven to 450 degrees (F). Using muffin pans put a small amount of oil (about 1/4 teaspoon each) in the bottom of 10 cups. If desired, put pieces of fat from beef in the bottom of the cups. The beef fat may not produce enough oil on its own, so it may still need a little oil in addition. Once the oven is preheated, put the pan in the oven for about 6 or 7 minutes or until fat renders and is very hot.

Pour the batter into the hot muffin cups to about 2/3 full, and return it to the oven to bake about 12-14 minutes until they finish puffing up. Do not open the oven during cooking. Turn down heat to 350 degrees (F) and bake until golden brown, about 7 or 8 minutes more. Remove from the oven, and serve warm with butter.

Pasta with Brie

Serves 4

Ingredients:

1 16-ounce package spaghetti or other pasta
1 13-ounce package Brie cheese
4 tablespoons butter
freshly ground pepper to taste

Directions:

Cut the butter and the Brie up into pieces to make melting it easier. Set aside and let come to room temperature.

Cook the pasta per the directions on the package. Drain and add back to the cooking pot.

Add the Brie and butter to the hot pasta, stir until melted, and stir in pepper to taste. Serve while hot.

Mushroom Risotto

The idea of risotto is to stir until the rice releases the starches and absorbs the liquids. It involves a lot of stirring, but it's so delicious!   Serves 4

Ingredients:

4-5 cups chicken stock or broth
3 tablespoons olive oil, divided
2 pounds cremini or wild mushrooms, chopped
3-4 shallots, diced (equiv. to 1 medium onion)
1 1/2 cups Arborio or other short grain rice
1/2 cup dry white wine or more to taste

salt to taste
freshly ground black pepper to taste
3 tablespoons finely chopped chives
4 tablespoons butter, plus more for frying
1 cup freshly grated Parmesan cheese

Directions:

In a large skillet over medium-high heat, heat about 2 tablespoons oil and some butter. Stir in the mushrooms, and cook until soft, about 3 minutes. Remove mushrooms and their liquid to a bowl, and set aside. In a small saucepan, heat the chicken stock.

Add some oil and butter to skillet, and stir in the shallots. Cook 1 minute. Add rice, stirring to coat with oil and butter, about 2 minutes. Continue stirring until rice has taken on a pale, golden color. Pour in wine, stirring constantly until the wine is fully absorbed. Add 1/2 cup hot broth to the rice, and stir until the broth is absorbed. Continue adding broth 1/2 cup at a time, stirring frequently, until the liquid is absorbed and the rice is cooked, about 15 to 20 minutes. The total cooking time for the rice is about 35-40 minutes.

Remove from heat, and stir in mushrooms with their liquid, butter, chives, and Parmesan. Add salt and pepper to taste. Serve immediately.

Spätzle

Similar to Italian gnocchi, Spätzle goes very well with Hungarian Goulash, but you can serve it as a side with any dish. Make the batter ahead, and let rest in the fridge until time to eat. Make the spätzle just in time to serve. Serves 4

Ingredients:

4 egg yolks
1 egg
1 3/4 cups milk
3 cups all-purpose flour
1/2 teaspoon salt
1/4 teaspoon freshly ground pepper
2 tablespoons butter
1 tablespoon fresh chopped parsley

Directions:

In a small bowl, beat together the egg yolks, egg, and milk. In a medium bowl, combine the flour, salt, and pepper. Add the egg mixture to the flour mixture, and mix by hand until well blended. Do not over-mix. If it seems too thick, you can add a little milk. If it seems too loose, you can add a little more flour. Cover the bowl, and refrigerate for at least 1 hour to allow the batter to rest.

In a large pan, add water and salt, and bring to a boil. Place a colander with large holes on top of the pot. Place the batter in the colander and with a spatula, force through the holes to form spätzle. Cook for 4 to 5 minutes, until they are cooked al dente. Use a strainer and drain well, and then transfer cooked spätzle to a frying pan.

Add butter to the frying pan and heat to medium. Add the cooked spätzle, and sauté until light golden brown. Sprinkle fresh parsley over them, and serve immediately.

Grilled Corn

Serves 4

Ingredients:

4 whole corn cobs
salted butter, melted
seasonings, see below

Directions:

Prepare grill. Heat to very hot- around 500 degrees (F). Remove husks and silk from the corn. Place on the grill, and close the lid. Every 2 minutes, turn the corn so that you get grill marks on all sides. They should only cook about 8-10 minutes total. Once the corn is cooked, brush with melted butter, and sprinkle with your seasoning as desired.

Paprika butter corn- Sprinkle a little paprika into the melted butter. Brush onto the corn and serve.

Mexican corn- After the corn is nearly cooked, brush with small amount of butter, then sprinkle crumbled queso fresco onto the corn. Garnish with chopped parsley and serve.

Chili-Lime corn- Mix together butter, 3/4 teaspoon chili powder, juice from 1/4 to 1/2 lime, and salt. After the corn is nearly cooked, brush with butter mixture.

Parmesan corn- After the corn is nearly cooked, brush with small amount of butter, then sprinkle fresh grated Parmesan onto the corn, and close the lid to melt. Garnish with chopped parsley and serve.

Steamed Artichokes

Fresh artichokes are simply delicious. We like them served with melted butter, a lemon aioli, or just plain mayonnaise to dip the leaves in.

Ingredients:

large artichokes (1 per person)

Lemon Aioli: Make ahead and refrigerate

1/2 cup mayonnaise (Best Foods or Hellmann's)
2 tablespoons juice from fresh lemon (to taste)

Directions:

Cut off the very tops of the artichokes using a large knife. Pluck off any small leaves on the outside and discard. Snip off the sharp ends from the remaining leaves using kitchen scissors. Trim the ends of the stems. Use a peeler and peel the outside off of the stems. Wash and put in a large pot, and add about 1-2 inches of water. Steam covered for about 45-50 minutes (for large artichokes), or until they are soft and a fork is easily inserted into the heart. Check to be sure the water does not run dry during cooking.

Use tongs and remove from the water. Hold upside down to drain out the water. Transfer to a plate or bowl and let cool. Once cool enough to handle, remove leaves, getting down to the center hair. Remove the hair and discard.

Dip the meaty end of the leaves in butter, aioli or mayo- it's delicious! Now eat your heart out!

Rosemary Potatoes

Serves 2

Ingredients:

    3/4 pound fingerling potatoes
    1/4 cup extra-virgin olive oil
    1-2 tablespoons butter, cut into pieces
    1/4 cup dried rosemary leaves
    1/4 teaspoon salt

Directions:

Wash and dry the potatoes. Cut the fingerlings in half, lengthwise.

Put dried rosemary leaves into a spice grinder, and grind to medium-fine. Toss the rosemary, the olive oil, and salt into a plastic bag. Add potatoes, and shake to coat.

Add the butter pieces to a non-stick frying pan and heat to medium. Put the potatoes cut side down and cook for 8-12 minutes, or until the potatoes are a deep golden brown on the bottoms. Turn the potatoes over and cook a few minutes more, or until they are cooked all the way through. The cooking time will vary depending on their size and how hot they are cooked at. Serve while hot.

If making this for a crowd, it would be simpler to use the same technique, except bake them in the oven at 425 degrees (F), for 25-30 minutes, turning them after 15 minutes. To save the mess, you could use foil to line a baking pan and coat it with olive oil to help prevent sticking.

Potatoes Au Gratin

Serves 4

Ingredients:

1 1/2 cups (6 ounces) grated sharp cheddar cheese
additional 1/2 cup cheese for top of casserole (optional)
2 large russet potatoes
1/2 large yellow onion
2 cups milk

6 tablespoons butter
3 tablespoons flour
salt to taste
freshly ground pepper to taste

Directions:

Preheat oven to 350°.

Butter the sides and bottom of an 8 x 8 inch deep baking dish.

Heat a saucepan to low heat. Add butter and melt. Sprinkle in the flour, and stir until the flour is fully incorporated and smooth. Slowly add the milk, and whisk to incorporate as you go. Slowly add the cheese (a bit at a time), stirring to incorporate as you go.

Cut potatoes into 1/8 to 1/4 inch slices. Cut onion into 1/8 inch slices, and separate into rings. Layer the pan with potatoes, onions, and then some sauce. Repeat until all of the ingredients are used up. Cover dish with foil, and bake around 35 minutes. Check to be sure the potatoes are nearly cooked. Uncover and sprinkle the additional cheese on top, and cook for 10 minutes longer. Let potatoes sit for 5 minutes before serving. Total cooking time will vary depending on the size and thickness of your baking dish.

Scalloped Potatoes with Onions

Serves 4

Ingredients:

1 1/2 pounds potatoes, thinly sliced
1 medium yellow onion, thinly sliced
salt and freshly ground pepper
4 tablespoons flour
3 tablespoons butter, diced
2 cups half and half as needed

Directions:

Preheat oven to 375 degrees (F). Butter the sides and bottom of an 8x8 inch baking dish.

Arrange one layer of potatoes in the bottom of the baking dish. Layer onion slices over the potatoes. Sprinkle the layer with salt and pepper, 1 tablespoon of the flour, and 1/4 of the butter. Repeat layering 3 more times, until all of the potatoes and onions have been used. Take the time to arrange the potatoes to fill gaps and pack it as tightly as possible.

Slowly pour half and half over the potatoes until they are just covered.

Bake until the potatoes are tender and the onions are soft, about 1 1/4 hours.

Cheese Puffs

Gruyère is the most common cheese used for the traditional French "Gougère". We've used sharp cheddar for this recipe, but Gruyère or another strong cheese could be used. Makes 30 to 40 small puffs.

Ingredients:

- 8 tablespoons salted butter (1 stick)
- 1 cup milk
- 1 cup all-purpose flour
- 4 extra-large eggs
- 1 egg for egg wash
- 6 ounces finely grated sharp cheddar cheese

Directions:

Preheat oven to 425 degrees (F). Line a baking sheet with parchment paper.

Using a medium sauce pan, heat the milk and butter over medium heat until scalded and the butter is melted. Turn heat to low. Add the flour all at once. Stir vigorously with a wooden spoon until the dough forms a ball. Continue stirring a minute or two until the ball becomes a little drier. Remove from heat.

Using a hand mixer, beat the eggs into the batter on medium speed one at a time, until each one is fully incorporated. Add the cheese and beat until incorporated.

Drop dough onto a baking sheet- about 1 1/4 inch in diameter, 3/4 inch high, and about 1 inch apart. Easiest might be a pastry bag, but you can use 2 spoons to get the dough on the sheet. To make a pastry bag, pour mixture into a plastic zip bag, and cut a small amount off one corner.

Beat the additional egg with 1 teaspoon water or milk to make a glaze. Lightly brush the tops of the puffs with glaze before baking. Bake for about 15 minutes, or until the puffs are soft in the middle and a light golden brown on the outside.

The best way to freeze cheese puffs is to drop extra dough onto a cookie sheet and pop the sheet into the freezer. When they are frozen, transfer them to a zip bag, getting out as much air as possible. You can bake them straight from the freezer- no need to defrost. Just give them a minute or two more in the oven.

Buttermilk Cornbread and Muffins

Makes 10-12 muffins or an 8-inch skillet. Dang good either way!

Ingredients:

Dry:
>   1/2 cup all-purpose flour
>   1 cup corn meal
>   4 teaspoons baking powder
>   1/2 teaspoon baking soda
>   1/2 teaspoon salt

Wet:
>   2 large eggs
>   1 cup buttermilk
>   4 tablespoons butter, melted
>   kernels and milk from one ear of corn (optional)
>   2 jalapeños chopped (optional)
>   oil for pan (avocado or other high-heat oil)

Directions:

Preheat oven to 425 degrees (F)

Mix together wet ingredients. In a separate larger bowl, mix the dry ingredients together. Add wet ingredients to the dry, and mix with a spoon. Do not over-mix.

If making muffins, put approximately 1/2 teaspoon oil in the bottom of each muffin tin cup. Place the tin in the oven to heat, about 3-5 minutes, or just until starting to smoke. Once the pan is hot, carefully spoon batter into the cups, and return the pan to the oven as quickly as possible. Bake for about 15-20 minutes, or until the muffins are set and browning on top.

If using a cast iron pan, preheat the pan for a 20 minutes, and then put approximately 2 tablespoons oil in the bottom of the pan. Carefully pour the batter into the pan, and return the pan to the oven. Bake about 20 minutes.

If using a corn stick pan, follow the same process, but bake about 10-15 minutes only.

Onion Rings

Serves 3-4

Ingredients:

2 large sweet onions (we like Walla Wallas)
1/2 cup flour
1/2 teaspoon baking powder
1/2 teaspoon salt
1 slightly beaten egg

1/2 cup milk
2 or more cups panko crumbs
oil for frying (peanut or avocado)
salt for seasoning

Directions:

Slice the onion into thick slices, and separate into rings when ready to begin making the onion rings (don't do this ahead).

Mix together flour, baking powder, salt, and set aside. In a separate dish, mix together egg and milk. Put panko crumbs in a separate dish. Coat all of the rings in the flour mixture and set aside. Mix some of the flour mixture in with the egg/milk a little at a time until you get a batter consistency. You can always add more milk, or more flour as needed to get the desired consistency.

Put about 1" of oil in a sauce pan, and heat to about 350-360 degrees (F). Once the oil is hot, you can begin frying.

Dip the floured onion rings into the batter, then dip them in the panko, taking care to coat them completely with crumbs.

Fry only a few at a time- cook on each side for a minute or two until golden brown, and then transfer them to a wire rack on a cookie sheet to drain and cool. Sprinkle with salt (or other seasoning as desired) as soon as they come out of the frying pan. They can be kept on the wire rack in a 225 degree (F) oven for a few minutes to keep warm until time to serve.

Fresh Herb Stuffing

John's Fresh Herb Stuffing comes out so well because of the amount of herbs he uses. He uses fresh rather than dried when he can get them, but dried herbs will otherwise do. Use 1/3 the amount if the herbs are dried.

1 recipe is about enough to stuff a 17 pound turkey. This can be used to stuff a bird, or can be made in an oven-proof pan. It is easy to make as a vegetarian option as well.

Ingredients:

3/4 loaf white bread
1 1/2 large yellow onions- chopped
1/2 head celery, including the leaves, chopped
2 sticks salted butter (8 ounces)
3 eggs, lightly beaten
1/2 cup chicken stock or broth, or more if desired

1/2 teaspoon freshly ground pepper
additional salt if desired
chopped fresh marjoram- 1/4 cup
chopped fresh oregano- 1/4 cup
chopped fresh thyme- 1/4 cup

Directions:

Lay the bread slices out on the counter for about an hour, turning over to dry out both sides. Cut the bread into 3/4 inch cubes. Melt butter in a large sauce pan. Add onions, celery, pepper, and herbs. Sauté until the onions and celery are soft. Pour the veggie and herb mixture into the bread. Add the eggs and stir. Add enough broth to get the stuffing to the right moistness- you don't want it too wet, but you don't want it dry. The amount you need will vary with how dry the bread is, how large the eggs are, etc.

If using inside a turkey, stuff and pin the ends closed. Don't pack the stuffing in too tight.

If baking in a dish, place the stuffing in a buttered oven-proof dish, and bake covered with foil in a 350 degree (F) oven for 20 minutes. Uncover and bake 15 minutes more to get some brown on top.

Baking Powder Biscuits

Serves 4 (Makes about 12 large biscuits)

Ingredients:

4 cups all-purpose flour
8 teaspoons baking powder
1 teaspoon salt

1 teaspoon cream of tartar
1/2 pound of cold butter, or 1 cup shortening
1 1/3 cups milk

Directions:

Preheat oven to 450 degrees (F).

In a large bowl, mix dry ingredients together well. If you don't have cream of tartar, you can use an extra teaspoon of baking powder as an option. Cut the butter into 1/4 or 1/2 inch cubes. Using a fork, cut the butter or shortening into the dry ingredients, until the butter or shortening pieces are the size of peas, but don't over mix. No need for them to be uniform in size either.

Form a well in the center of the bowl. Add the milk in all at once. Using your hands, mix the dry ingredient/ butter mixture into the center, until all of it is moist. Do not over mix.

Flour a work surface, and dump the contents of the bowl out on the surface. Using your hands, mix any that is not incorporated into the dough. Roll or pat the dough flat to about 1 inch thick. Use a clean glass as a cookie cutter, just put a little flour on it to prevent the dough from sticking. Cut out biscuits and put on an ungreased cookie sheet, not touching each other. Use the scraps of dough to make more biscuits. The less you work the dough, the more flakey it will be.

Paint a little milk or cream over the top of the biscuits to help them get golden on top. Bake at 450 degrees (F). Thinner ones (inch thick) will only take about 10 minutes, while thicker ones will take around 12 or 13 minutes. Serve while hot with butter and jam.

Mac and Cheese

Mac and Cheese used to be our kids' favorite side dish. Adding a little of hot paprika for a little extra zip makes it extra tasty! We like to experiment with different cheeses. If we use other cheeses or a mix of cheeses, we like to go for something with more flavor than jack or mozzarella. Fontina, Gruyère, and sharp white cheddar all work well. We sometimes add chopped roasted chilis to the Mac and Cheese, and that is super good. But you could add cooked crab or lobster, or any nearly cooked vegetable. The possibilities are endless!

Serves 4

Ingredients:

2 cups uncooked macaroni or other pasta

1/2 teaspoon hot paprika or cayenne (optional)

4 tablespoons butter

2 cups grated cheese

2 cups milk

2 tablespoons flour

1/4 cup bread crumbs

2 tablespoons butter for topping

Directions:

Cook the pasta per the instructions on the package, except do not fully cook. It should be very al dente. Pasta will continue to cook once the Mac and Cheese if assembled and baked. Drain and set pasta aside.

Heat a saucepan to low heat. Add butter and melt. Sprinkle in the flour, and stir until the flour is fully incorporated and smooth. Slowly add the milk, and whisk to incorporate as you go. Slowly add the cheese (a bit at a time), stirring to incorporate as you go. Add paprika or cayenne if using. If the sauce seems too thick, add a little more milk. If it seems too loose, add a little more cheese. Add the cooked pasta to the sauce, and pour into an 8 x 8 baking pan.

To make the topping, melt butter in a small bowl, and add the breadcrumbs. Mix, and sprinkle the bread crumbs over the top of the Mac and Cheese. Bake at 350 degrees (F) for about 20-30 minutes, or until it browns a little on top and is bubbling inside.

Spicy Cowboy Beans

John makes his beans enough to have some for dinner tonight, and some to freeze. They work out marvelously to freeze in portion sizes to pull out for lunch, or as a dinner side. This size recipe will serve lots! 1/2 of this recipe will serve 4 as a side dish.

Ingredients:

2 cups pinto beans
4 andouille sausages, sliced
1 ham hock bone
6 ounces ham, diced
4 strips bacon
1 large onion
6-8 cloves garlic
4 tablespoons Mexi-Mix Seasoning (see recipe)
3 large jalapeño peppers, chopped
1 12-ounce lager beer
2-3 ribs celery, diced
3 bay leaves
1 small can tomato paste

Directions:

Boil the beans for 1 hour covered in water, then set aside until the water is cool. Drain the water, and set beans aside. Alternately, you can soak them in water overnight, then drain. In a large pot, sauté the bacon until rendered. Add the ham and andouille, sauté until brown, and remove from the pan. Add the onion, garlic, celery, and jalapeños to the pan, and sauté until softened. Add the tomato paste, beer, meats, and seasonings into the veggie mixture, and bring to a boil. Stir in the beans. Add water to cover the beans by an inch. You may have to add water during the cooking to be sure it's enough to fully cook the beans.

Cook covered until the beans are tender. This will take 2-4 hours depending on the type of beans. If there seems to be excess liquid at the end of cooking, simply remove the lid and boil liquid off. If soaked overnight, the beans could cook more quickly.

Pasta with Anchovies

Serves 4

Ingredients:

- 1 pound of rotini pasta
- 1 can anchovies
- 4 tablespoons butter, cut into pieces

Directions:

Make the pasta per the instructions on the package. Drain the anchovy oil into a large mixing bowl, and chop the anchovies. Add anchovies and butter pieces to the bowl. Drain the pasta, and add to the bowl, adding a bit of pasta water as well. Let sit a minute or two while the butter melts.

Stir and serve immediately.

Homemade Sauerkraut

This naturally fermented sauerkraut is super healthy not to mention yummy. It's excellent to use for Reuben Sandwiches (see recipe) or hot dogs.

Ingredients:

1/2-3/4 medium sized head of cabbage
2 teaspoons salt
wide mouth quart mason jar, with airlock lid
-or- cheesecloth (4 layers) and rubber band to cover.

Directions:

Slice cabbage so that you end up with long shreds. Do not worry about having some thicker and some thinner- the extra texture makes this even better. Place the cabbage in a very large bowl, sprinkle in the salt, and mix thoroughly with clean hands. Let sit in the bowl 3-4 hours, until liquid begins to emerge and the cabbage starts to wilt a bit.

Fill a quart jar with the cabbage and any liquid that accumulated. Mash down gently (don't want to bruise the cabbage), and try to get as much air out as possible. Use a glass *Pickle Pebble* or a plastic bag filled with water and sealed, to weigh down the cabbage.

Cover jar with the airlock lid or cheesecloth folded in 4 layers with rubber band, and let sit out on the counter until it's how sour you like it. If after 24 hours, the liquid has not covered all of the cabbage, add water over the cabbage until it's fully submersed in liquid.

After about 5 days, taste periodically using a clean utensil each time. You may want to place the jar in a dish in case the liquid level grows and overflows, if the jar was packed full. Since this is naturally fermented, any bacteria on the cabbage, the jar, or utensils could disrupt the process and make it go bad. Once it smells and tastes like sauerkraut, you're good to go.

Once it is to your liking, store in the fridge covered with the jar lid. Refrigeration greatly slows the fermentation process. Kept in a jar, it will keep for a month or more. Once you try it, you won't believe how simple and delicious it is. Enjoy!

Cauliflower with Cheddar Cheese Sauce

Serves 4

Ingredients:

1/2 head of cauliflower
2 tablespoons butter
1 tablespoon flour
1/2 cup milk
1 cup grated cheddar cheese
2 tablespoons bread crumbs
1 tablespoon butter for topping
pinch hot paprika or cayenne powder(optional)

Directions:

Cut cauliflower into desired size florets. In a large pan with a lid, put about 3/4 inch of water in the bottom of the pan, and add cauliflower. Cover and bring to a boil, and then turn down to medium-low heat. Cook 5-7 minutes, until the cauliflower is getting to be fork tender, but not soft. It will cook a little more when you bake the dish. Drain the water out and set aside.

Heat a saucepan to low heat. Add butter and melt. Sprinkle in the flour, and stir until the flour is fully incorporated and smooth. Slowly add the milk, and whisk to incorporate as you go. Slowly add the cheese (a bit at a time), stirring to incorporate as you go. Stir in a pinch of cayenne or paprika if desired.

Add the cooked cauliflower to the sauce, and pour into an 8 x 8 baking pan.

To make the topping, melt butter in a small bowl, and add the breadcrumbs. Mix and sprinkle the bread crumbs over the top of the cauliflower.

Bake at 350 degrees (F) for about 20-30 minutes, or until it browns a little on top and is bubbling inside.

Other veggies can be used for this recipe, such as broccoli.

Mexican Sautéed Mixed Vegetables

This makes a great fresh side dish for any Mexican food meal.

Serves 4

Ingredients:

1 fresh red pepper
3 ears fresh corn
3 large jalapeños
extra virgin olive oil for frying
salt to taste

Directions:

Cut the corn kernels off of the cob. Seed, core and dice the jalapeños and red pepper. The vegetable pieces should be roughly the same size for even cooking.

Sauté until just getting to be soft, then remove from heat. The veggies should be firm and not overcooked. Serve immediately.

Mexican Rice

Ingredients:

1 cup long grain rice
1 1/2 cup chicken stock or broth
1/2 cup water
3/4 cup Fresh Salsa (see recipe), or jar as desired
1 teaspoon Mexi-Mix Seasoning (see recipe)
salt as desired

Directions:

Add salsa, chicken stock, and water to a saucepan with lid. Stir in the seasonings, and bring to a boil. Once boiling, add rice, stir once, cover, and turn heat to low. Let steam on low for 20 minutes, or until rice is fully cooked and the moisture is absorbed. The amount of water you use may vary depending on how much moisture is in the salsa. Also, if using chicken stock that is already salted, additional salt may not be needed. We tend to not salt our stock very much, and then add salt to each dish as appropriate.

Fresh Mango Salsa

Ingredients:

1 large ripe mango, peeled and seeded
1/8 to 1/4 of a whole ripe pineapple, peeled and cored
1/4 of a large sweet onion or red onion
2 jalapeños, seeded and stemmed
1/4 bunch cilantro, chopped
juice of 1/2 lime or orange
pinch of salt, to taste
corn tortilla chips for serving

Directions:

Chop the washed, peeled, and seeded ingredients into a bowl. Add lime or orange juice, salt, and then stir. Serve right away, or store in fridge up to a couple hours before serving.

If the mango and pineapple are very ripe, using lime balances the sweet well. If either the mango or pineapples are not quite as ripe as you hoped, then using a sweet orange instead of lime works well.

This makes a great appetizer, or goes really well with a Mexican food feast.

Pico de Gallo

We first had this style of pico de gallo in Tucson, Arizona in 1995. We went to a Mexican fast food restaurant and ordered tacos 'to go'. They were so good, we decided to make them like this at home.

Serve with chips as an appetizer, or put on tacos instead of lettuce, tomato, and onion. Super fresh tasting!

Serves 4

Ingredients:

    1 ripe tomato, chopped
    1/2 large cucumber, seeded and chopped
    1/4 med sweet onion, chopped
    1/4 bunch fresh cilantro, chopped
    juice from 1/2 lime
    salt to taste

Directions:

Mix the ingredients together. Let it sit for an hour or two before serving to let the flavors blend. Serve with tortilla chips or with any Mexican dish.

Guacamole

We love guacamole and tortilla chips as an appetizer, or to serve with any Mexican food meal. Delicious!

Serves 4

Ingredients:

2 ripe avocados
1/4 bunch cilantro minced
1/4 ripe tomato, finely chopped
1/4 small sweet onion finely chopped
juice of 1/4 lime
1/4 to 1/2 teaspoon chili powder
1/4 teaspoon cumin
1/4 teaspoon salt
1/4 teaspoon Tabasco (or to taste)

Directions:

Put avocados in a mixing bowl, and mash until as smooth as you'd like it. We like ours with a few chunks. Stir in the rest of the ingredients until mixed. Guac can be made ahead and refrigerated until ready to use. If making ahead, put plastic wrap over it with no air between the wrap and the guacamole to help keep it from turning brown.

Fresh Salsa

You can use fresh vine-ripened tomatoes for this, Romas work the best. We have a hard time getting the nice ripe tomatoes with lots of flavor year round, so we substitute canned tomatoes in this case.

Ingredients:

2 pounds fresh ripe tomatoes
-or- 1 28-ounce can diced tomatoes, including juice
1/4 to 1/2 cup cilantro, leaves and stems, chopped
1/2 poblano pepper, roasted, peeled and chopped
1 1/2 to 3 jalapeños, seeded and finely chopped
1/2 cup finely chopped yellow onion

3 green onions, chopped
1-2 cloves finely minced garlic
1/4 teaspoon cumin
1/2 teaspoon salt, or more to taste
1/4 teaspoon freshly ground pepper
2 tablespoons fresh lime juice

Directions:

If using fresh tomatoes, blanch them until the skin splits- a minute or less. When cool enough to handle, remove the skin and the seeds and any hard core pieces.

Add the tomatoes to the food processor. Whir until smooth. Add the rest of the ingredients, and whir until everything is chopped to your desired consistency. Refrigerate for at least 2 hours before serving. It's even better the next day!

Keep unused salsa in a glass jar in the fridge for up to a week.

Cooked Salsa

Serve with tortilla chips or with your Mexican meal. When we can get vine-ripened plum tomatoes, we like to use those instead of the canned.

Serves 4

Ingredients:

1 14-ounce can tomatoes, chopped and with juice
  -or- 1 pound ripe plum tomatoes, skinned and seeded
1 clove garlic, minced
1/4 cup cilantro stems, minced
1/4 cup cilantro leaves, chopped
1 jalapeño finely chopped
1/2 cup yellow onion, finely chopped
1 teaspoon chili powder
1/3 teaspoon cumin
1/4 teaspoon salt
1/4 teaspoon Tabasco (or to taste)

Directions:

Put everything into a saucepan except 1/2 of the jalapeños, 1/2 of the onions, and the cilantro leaves. Simmer just until slightly thickened. Use blender, food processor, or stick blender to make smooth consistency. Add the remaining jalapeño, onion, and cilantro leaves.

Refrigerate for a few hours before serving.

Pickled Jalapeños

This could not be simpler to make, and the cost is next to nothing if you've already got a few canning jars. Once they are canned, they can last on the shelf (sealed) for months. Once open, refrigerate them, and they will last for a month or more in the fridge. The jalapeños need to sit in the brine for a couple of weeks to become fully pickled. Once pickled, they are delicious!

Note: Be sure to wear gloves while handling the jalapeños.

Ingredients:

about 15 large fresh jalapeños
3 pint jars with lids, sterilized
2 medium sized carrots

2 cups white vinegar
2 cups water
1/4 cup salt

Directions:

Wash the jalapeños, and peel the carrots. Cut the carrots into about 1/8 inch slices. Cut the jalapeños less-thin than the carrots, around 1/4 inch thick slices. Pack the jars with jalapeños, layering in some carrots. Try to pack them tightly without bruising the peppers. Leave about 1/2 inch of room at the top of the jar.

Heat the vinegar, water, and salt to a rolling boil. Place the jars on a dish towel someplace where they can sit until they cool. Ladle the boiling liquid into the jars, filling to about 1/4 inch from the top. Some airspace is needed for them to properly seal. The peppers might float, that's OK. Put the lids on the canning jars and tighten. Let sit on the counter until fully cooled- a couple of hours at least. Hopefully, if the liquid was hot enough, each jar will seal.

You can tell if it's sealed by the lid becoming concave (looks bowed inward), rather than convex (looks bowed outward) as they were when you first put the lid on. Sometimes you can hear a pop sound when they seal, but not always. Not hearing the pop does not mean it's not sealed. If one of your jars did not seal, don't worry. Just put that one in the fridge, and use it first!

As always with home canned goods, never use the jar if the color, odor, or texture is not right. Also if it's cloudy or not sealed when you open it, toss it out.

Pad Thai

Pad Thai can be made as a side dish for a Thai meal, or you could add chicken or pork and have it as a main dish. Either way, it's delicious! Both tamarind pods and tamarind paste can typically be found at an Asian grocery store. Serves 2-3

Ingredients:

6-8 ounces (1/2 package) rice noodles
4 cloves minced garlic
3 eggs, lightly beaten
1 cup bean sprouts
3 green onions, chopped
1/2 cup peanuts
oil for stir frying (peanut or avocado)

Sauce:

1/4 cup fish sauce
6 tamarind pods + 3/4 cup water
-or- 3 tablespoons tamarind paste + 1/2 cup water
2 tablespoons rice vinegar
1/4 cup brown sugar

Directions:

Bring water to a boil. To make the tamarind liquid, open the tamarind pods, pull out the veins and outer pods and discard. Add the inner pods to a heat-proof bowl, and pour in boiling water. Let sit until the paste can be separated from the seeds. Discard the seeds. Mix the paste with the water until it's a smooth liquid, whether using pods or store-bought paste. Add fish sauce, vinegar, and brown sugar to the tamarind liquid and mix well. Set sauce aside.

Soak the rice noodles in a large bowl of hot tap water for 30 minutes before stir frying.

Heat wok to medium-high heat, and then add the oil. Add the garlic to the wok, and immediately add the noodles and two-thirds of the sauce. Continuously stir fry, until the garlic and noodles are cooked and the sauce is boiling. If at this point you feel it needs more sauce, add the remaining sauce. Add the bean sprouts and stir fry for about 1 minute.

At the end, add the beaten egg by swirling it over the noodles. Meanwhile also add the green onions and peanuts. Stir fry until the egg is cooked.

Gyoza (Pot Stickers) with Dipping Sauce

Ingredients:

3/4 pound ground pork
2 cups Napa cabbage, chopped
2 green onions, minced
1 medium carrot, grated
1 clove garlic, minced
1 1/2 tablespoons fresh ginger, minced
salt and pepper to taste
2 tablespoons cornstarch
1 tablespoon low sodium soy sauce
1 tablespoon sesame oil
1 10-ounce package round gyoza wrappers
oil to cook; avocado or peanut
1 cup chicken stock or broth

Dipping Sauce:

2 tablespoons low sodium soy sauce
2 tablespoons water
1 tablespoon rice vinegar
1 tablespoon green onion, chopped
1 tablespoon fresh ginger, grated
1/2 teaspoon red chili flakes
1/4 teaspoon sesame oil

Makes approx. 40 gyoza; some for tonight and some to freeze for quick appetizers!

Directions:

Mix together Dipping Sauce ingredients and set aside. For the Gyoza, combine pork, cabbage, carrot, green onions, garlic, ginger, salt, pepper, cornstarch, sesame oil, and soy sauce.

Place a spoonful of filling in center of wrapper, brush around the edge of wrapper lightly with water, and close pot sticker. Press firmly or use your fingers to pinch edges together. Place them on a plate vertically. Keep the plate covered as you work with plastic wrap to prevent them from drying out. Once all the wrappers are filled, you can freeze some if desired. Just place them on a cookie sheet not touching each other, and cover with plastic. Once frozen, transfer to a zip bag and keep in the freezer until needed. Just pull out as many you want, thaw then cook per the directions.

To cook, add oil to pan, then add 1/4 inch of chicken broth to the pan. Add gyoza, not touching each other. Simmer covered for 5 minutes to steam, then uncover and simmer until the broth boils off, and oil browns the bottoms of gyoza. Before the broth is fully boiled off, be sure they seem cooked inside-they should be firm at this point. If needed, you can add just a little more broth.

Fried Spring Rolls

Ingredients:

Meat Marinade (Marinate for 10 mins)
   1/2-1 pound ground or finely chopped chicken or pork
   1 tablespoon soy sauce
   freshly ground black pepper

Other ingredients:
   1 tablespoon cornstarch
   1/4 cup water
   1 package spring roll wrappers, defrosted
   oil, for deep frying
   sweet chili sauce for dipping

Filling:
   2 tablespoons cooking oil, divided
   4 tablespoons garlic, finely minced
   4 tablespoons fresh ginger, finely minced
   'some' bean sprouts
   1-2 green onions, chopped
   1/3 small head of cabbage, shredded
   1-2 carrots, thin julienne cut
   1 tablespoons fish sauce

Directions:

Heat a wok over medium-high heat. When hot, swirl in just 1 tablespoon of the cooking oil. Stir fry the meat until browned. Remove browned meat from wok to a bowl and set aside. Wipe the wok clean, and return to med-high heat. When just starting to get hot, swirl in the remaining cooking oil. When hot, add in the carrots and cabbage, and stir fry for about a minute. Add in the green onion, garlic, ginger, and then the sprouts. Continuously stir fry for about 2 minutes, or until the carrots have softened. Add back in the meat, the fish sauce, and toss again.

Spread the mixture out on a baking sheet to let cool. Prop up the baking sheet on one end so that any liquid collects on the other side. When the mixture is cool, discard the liquid.

In a small bowl, whisk together the cornstarch and water. This is your slurry to seal the spring rolls. Open the spring roll wrapper package, cover with plastic wrap to prevent drying out.

Add 2 tablespoons of filling and meat to a spring roll wrapper, and roll up as tightly as possible, using the cornstarch slurry to glue edges down. Keep rolled spring rolls covered with plastic wrap to prevent drying while you work.

When ready to fry, heat at least 1/2 inch of oil in a wok or deep pan to 350 degrees (F). Carefully fry few at a time, turning to brown evenly. They will fry for very short time (less than 3 minutes). Let cool on rack. They can be moved to a 225 degree (F) oven to keep warm for a little bit until dinner time.

You can freeze spring rolls prior to cooking in oil, just freeze individually, then store in air tight manner. Thaw before cooking. It works perfectly to grab a few for a quick delicious appetizer!!

We typically find these spring roll wrappers in the frozen section of an Asian food store. Just thaw them before using. Be sure to keep them covered with plastic wrap while you work to prevent them from drying out. You can refreeze any that are left over, no problem.

Korean Kimchi

Ingredients:

4 heads of choi sum or baby bok choi
2 tablespoons salt
2 cloves finely minced or grated garlic
1 teaspoon finely minced or grated ginger
3-4 green onions cut into 1-inch pieces
2-4 tablespoons gochugaru powder (spicy chili powder)
1 tablespoon fish sauce
wide-mouth jar with airlock lid
-or- cheesecloth and rubber band
optional- julienned daikon or sliced radishes

Directions:

Trim and discard the thick base of the choi, separating all the stalks. If the stalks are big, cut in half lengthwise, keeping leaves and stems together. Place in a large bowl. Sprinkle with salt, and toss together. Let stand for 3-4 hours, or until the won bok is wilted and has lost some crunchiness.

Drain the choi in a colander and rinse, tossing well under the water to remove the salt. Drain and return to a large bowl.

Add remaining ingredients and mix well. Pack kimchi into a quart jar with airlock lid if you've got it, or cover with cheesecloth and put rubber band around the jar. Let stand on the kitchen counter for a day before refrigerating. If you want it to sour quickly, do not refrigerate- leave on the counter for another day. It will be sour within a couple of days. Taste with a clean spoon, and when you think it's done, put the normal lid on and refrigerate.

Note: Chlorine in water can inhibit the fermentation.

Korean Kimchi Pancakes (Kimchijeon)

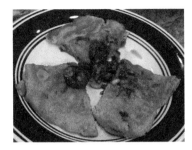  

Serves 2-4

Ingredients:

3 large eggs
1 1/2 tablespoons flour
pinch of salt
2 green onions, chopped
1 garlic clove, finely chopped
1 teaspoon ginger, finely chopped
1 cup kimchi, chopped, with its juice
butter for frying

Dipping Sauce:

4 tablespoons soy sauce
2 tablespoons rice vinegar
1/2 teaspoon sesame oil
1 teaspoon toasted sesame seeds
1/4 very thinly sliced jalapeño (optional)
1-2 tablespoons green onion finely chopped

Directions:

In a small bowl, whisk together dipping sauce ingredients and set aside. In a separate bowl, whisk the eggs. Add the flour, and whisk until smooth. Stir in salt, green onion, garlic, ginger, and kimchi.

Heat a non-stick pan to medium. Melt butter, and then add 1/4 of the batter. Use a spatula to nudge the edges of the egg so it doesn't spread out too far. Use the spatula to spread the kimchi around in the pancake. Cook the pancake 2 to 3 minutes, until the edges are firm and the bottom is lightly browned. Flip the pancake over, and cook 2 to 3 minutes more until lightly browned. Add more butter as needed. Do this for the remaining pancakes. Serve the pancakes hot with the dipping sauce.

It's OK to make the dipping sauce and batter a little while ahead and let sit while you prepare the rest of the meal, but the pancakes should be made just ahead of serving.

Korean Green Onion Pancakes (Pajeon)

Serves 4 (makes 2 pancakes)

Ingredients:

2 tablespoons flour
1/4 teaspoon salt
4 large eggs, lightly beaten
1 bunch of green onions
1 clove garlic, finely chopped
1 teaspoon ginger, finely chopped
2 teaspoon soy sauce
oil for frying

Dipping Sauce: Make ahead and let sit:

4 tablespoons soy sauce
2 tablespoon rice vinegar
1/2 teaspoon sesame oil
1 teaspoon of toasted sesame seeds
1/4 very thinly sliced jalapeño (optional)
1-2 tablespoons finely chopped green onion

Directions:

Stir together the flour, salt, and eggs just until mixed. Cut the green onions into 3" lengths.

Heat oil in a non-stick pan. Fry the green onions white parts first, and then add the green parts, since the white parts take longer to cook. Cook until they're not quite cooked through, then add the garlic and ginger. Add the soy sauce to the pan when they're almost done. If using other ingredients, such as chilis, kimchi, or prawns, add them now and toss a few times to heat them through. Transfer to a dish and set aside.

Put 1/2 of the green onions in the pan, and pour 1/2 of the pancake batter over them, spreading the batter, and cook a few minutes until the bottom is nice and brown underneath, and the egg is firm near the edges. Using a wide spatula, flip the pancake, and cook for another minute or two until the egg is set and preferably crispy at the edges. Slide pancake onto a cutting board. Cut into six or eight wedges, and serve with dipping sauce. Repeat with remaining onions and batter.

Bibimbap

This can be served with Korean BBQ Kalbi Beef Ribs (see recipe)

Ingredients:

2 cups steamed white rice
1 carrot, julienned
a few green onions, julienned
bean sprouts
4 shiitake or other mushrooms, thinly sliced
3 cloves garlic
1 tablespoon black sesame seeds
1 tablespoon sesame oil
soy sauce, to taste
gochujang paste or other hot sauce
1 egg, cooked over easy

Directions:

Stir fry veggie ingredients separately with garlic, arranging on a serving plate to be able to make individual bibimbap bowls, or on arrange on top of a shared dish.

Add a tablespoon of oil into the bottom of a cast iron fry pan or wok, add the rice and cook on medium heat, until brown on the bottom.

If using a cast iron pan, you can use that for serving. Place veggies on top of rice, but place separately so you can see each ingredient beautifully placed on the rice. Put egg on top. Sprinkle with sesame seeds, and drizzle with sesame oil and soy sauce. Serve with gochujang or other hot sauce.

Cashew Chicken Vietnamese Spring Rolls

This makes a great make-ahead healthy side dish or snack. Bean sprouts inside also work nicely for these. Serves 4-6

Ingredients:

1 boneless/ skinless chicken breast (or shrimp)

2 ounces vermicelli noodles

1 clove garlic, minced

1/8 teaspoon crushed red peppers (optional)

1-2 cups finely shredded Napa cabbage

1 medium carrot, coarsely grated

2-3 green onions, chopped

1/4 cup fresh cilantro leaves

1 tablespoon sesame oil

2 tablespoons chopped dry-roasted cashews

2 tablespoon rice vinegar

2 teaspoons packed brown sugar

2 teaspoons soy sauce

2 teaspoons grated ginger

6 8-inch round rice papers

sweet chili sauce for dipping

Directions:

Cut chicken into 1/2 inch pieces. Using a wok, stir fry chicken, garlic, and pepper flakes in sesame oil until chicken is cooked through. Remove from heat and let cool. Dice into small pieces and set aside. Cook vermicelli in boiling water for 2-3 minutes, or just until tender. Drain. Rinse under cold water, and drain well. Use kitchen scissors and chop into small pieces. Combine cooked vermicelli and chicken with the shredded cabbage, carrot, green onions, cilantro, and cashews.

In small bowl, combine rice vinegar, brown sugar, soy sauce, and ginger. Add the amount needed of dressing to cabbage mix, and toss to coat.

Fill a large skillet about 1/2 full with water. Bring just to simmering, and then remove from heat. Place rice paper in the skillet, one at a time. Push it down gently to cover with water. Allow to soften, just a few seconds. Using tongs, lift rice paper, drain, and place on a dinner plate. Fill with small amount of filling on lower third of the paper, tightly roll up, and place on a clean/dry plate. Consider putting cilantro leaves with short stems, red pepper flakes, or shrimp on the rice paper just before the final turn to close it, since the rice papers are translucent.

Do this for the remaining rolls. Cover with plastic wrap and refrigerate. Serve with sweet chili sauce for dipping.

Spanakopitas

Ingredients:

1/3 cup yellow onion, finely chopped

1 10-ounce package frozen chopped spinach

5 ounces feta cheese, crumbled

3 green onions, chopped

2 tablespoons chopped parsley

3/4 cup ricotta cheese

2 eggs, lightly beaten

freshly ground pepper to taste

1/2 16-ounce package phyllo dough, thawed

melted salted butter as needed (about 1/4 pound)

Directions:

Thaw the spinach, and squeeze the water out. In a large saucepan over medium heat, slowly sauté onions until softened. Mix in spinach, parsley, and green onions. Cook approximately 10 minutes, or until most of the moisture has evaporated. Remove from heat. Mix in feta and ricotta cheeses, eggs, and pepper. Set aside.

Separate one sheet of phyllo from the stack and evenly dab with a light coating of butter. Place two more sheets of phyllo over the first, and butter each sheet lightly pressing the sheets together as you go. Cut the layered phyllo dough into 3 or 4 long strips lengthwise, depending on how big you want the spanakopitas. Keep the remaining phyllo covered with plastic wrap to keep it from drying out. Phyllo can be tricky to work with, as it is super thin. It's OK if some tears- the 1/2 package is plenty to accommodate this.

Lay out one strip of layered phyllo at a time on your work surface with one of the narrow ends close to you. Place filling up to the edge on the end closest to you in a triangle shape. Fold the bottom right corner over the filling to the left edge to form a triangle. Turn the lower left corner over to touch the right edge, trying to not leave air pockets. Continue turning the triangle over in this manner until you reach the end of the phyllo. Use a little butter to 'glue' the end down. Repeat with the remaining filling and phyllo dough.

Place filled phyllo dough triangles on a large baking sheet that has been lightly oiled. Brush with the remaining butter. It's OK to make them ahead and just bake when ready, but be sure to keep them covered with plastic wrap until ready to bake. Bake in a preheated 350 degree (F) oven, until golden brown, 45 to 55 minutes. They can be frozen, covered, before baking. Just thaw when ready to use.

Pita Bread

Makes 6 pitas

Ingredients:

1 teaspoon active dry yeast
1 cup warm water – about 110-115 degrees (F)
2 cups all-purpose flour
1/4 teaspoon salt
1/2 tablespoon olive oil

Directions:

Add warm water and olive oil to a measuring cup. Set aside.

Add flour, salt, and yeast to a food processor bowl. Whir to mix, and then pour in the water/ olive oil mixture. Whir it until it forms a ball, then keep whirring it for an additional 30 seconds. If it seems too wet, add a little more flour. If it doesn't come together in 1 ball, add more water. Place into lightly oiled bowl, cover with a clean towel, and let rise until doubled in size (approximately 2 hours).

Preheat the oven to 500 degrees (F) with pizza stone in the oven, and placed in the center of the oven.

Flour your work surface. Separate dough into 6 pieces. One or two at a time, gently roll out each piece using flour to prevent sticking. Gently move them onto the pizza stone, and cook on both sides to desired doneness. Transfer to a basket or plate, and cover with a clean towel while you cook the remaining pita. Serve while hot. If desired, after they are cooked, you can pan-fry them in a little olive oil, and sprinkle with Greek Seasoning (see recipe).

Greek Lemon Rice

Serves 4

Ingredients:

    1 cup long grain rice
    1/2 cup yellow onion- chopped
    2 tablespoons olive oil
    pinch salt, or to taste
    4 tablespoons juice from fresh lemon
    2 cups chicken stock or broth

Directions:

Heat a saucepan with a lid over medium heat. Add oil. When hot, add rice and chopped onions, and sauté until the onions are soft and the rice is turning golden brown, stirring often so it doesn't stick or burn. Add salt and lemon juice to rice, and sauté 1 minute more.

Add chicken broth to the rice. Let it come to a boil, and then reduce heat to low and cover. Cook until the rice is done and the liquid is absorbed, about 20 minutes. Then it's ready to serve!

Variation- to this recipe add:
    2 tablespoons chopped spaghetti pasta (uncooked)
    2 tablespoons finely chopped parsley

Sauté pasta along with rice, and proceed with recipe above. Stir in parsley after rice is cooked to make a pilaf.

Hummus

We first got this recipe from Aunt Georgie in 1992. When she served it to us at their house in California, she served it with lots of kinds of veggies cut small. Just perfect for an appetizer! We make ours slightly different than she, but in either case, it's great! Makes approximately 2 cups.

Ingredients:

1 15-ounce can chickpeas
1/4 cup juice from fresh lemon
1/2 cup roasted tahini (not raw)
2 medium cloves garlic, rough chopped
1-2 teaspoons soy sauce
1/8 teaspoon freshly ground pepper

For Garnish:
1 tablespoon fresh parsley, finely chopped
-or- 1 green onion, thinly sliced
-or- Kalamata olives and olive oil

Directions:

Drain the peas, saving the broth. Put peas, lemon juice, tahini, garlic, soy, and pepper into a blender. Blend until smooth, but not overly smooth. Add some pea broth if needed to help it blend.

Place into a serving bowl and refrigerate for at least 3 hours. It's even better refrigerated overnight.

When ready to serve, sprinkle fresh parsley and/or green onions on top. Alternately, you can put Kalamata olives and olive oil on top- goes great with a Greek feast.

Serve with any number of veggies cut small, and/or pita bread.

Tzatziki

We like tzatziki on gyros and souvlaki, or as an appetizer served with pita wedges. This needs to be made ahead of time to let the flavors blend.

Serves 4 or more

Ingredients:

    2 cups plain Greek yogurt
    2 tablespoons fresh dill, chopped
    1/2 teaspoon salt
    1 cup cucumber, grated medium (about 1 cuke)
    2 cloves garlic
    2 tablespoons lemon
    freshly ground pepper to taste

Directions:

Peel the cucumber, cut in half lengthwise, and remove seeds. Lay some paper towels on the counter, and grate the cucumber over them. Put one half of the grated cuke to a blender. Use the paper towels to pat the excess water out of the other half of the cucumber. Further chop the remaining grated cucumber if a finer texture is desired, and put into a mixing bowl.

Chop the garlic, and add to the blender. Add the yogurt to the blender, as well as the lemon, salt, and pepper, and mix well. Add blended yogurt mix to the bowl, and mix with remaining cuke. Add dill, and stir well.

Refrigerate at least several hours before serving. It really needs to let the flavors blend and the raw garlic mellow.

Naan

Makes 6 pieces

Ingredients:

3/4 cup warm water

2 tablespoons extra virgin olive oil

3 tablespoons plain yogurt

2 cups flour, plus more for kneading

1 teaspoons dried active yeast

1 teaspoon salt

1/8 teaspoon baking powder

Directions:

Be sure rack is in the middle of the oven, and preheat oven to 450 degrees (F) with a pizza stone in it.

Add flour, salt, baking powder, and yeast to a large bowl, and mix together. Add the warm water, yogurt, and olive oil to a separate container, and mix together. Pour the yogurt mixture into the flour mixture all at once. Stir until fully mixed together. It will be very sticky. Flour your work surface, and scrape the dough onto it. Kneed just until it forms a ball, adding flour as needed to help it not stick. Place the dough into a well-oiled bowl, and cover with a clean towel. Let rise in a warm place until doubled in size (approximately 1-2 hours).

Divide the dough into 6 pieces, and use a rolling pin to roll each piece to about 1/4 inch thick on a floured surface, working the dough as little as possible. Gently move the flattened pieces onto the pizza stone, and cook to desired doneness. Serve immediately.

Raita

This is a nice cool sauce that goes well with Chicken Tikka Masala and various curries (see recipes).

Ingredients:

1 cup Greek yogurt
1 cup cucumber – seeds removed, finely grated
1/4 teaspoon salt
5 teaspoons juice from fresh lemon
3/4 teaspoon dried mint
1 tablespoon dried dill leaves

Directions:

Grate cucumber. Using paper towels, dry the grated cucumber, then chop a little finer. Mix all of the rest of the ingredients. It is better if it is let sit in the fridge for a couple of hours before serving.

Another option is to put half of the grated cucumber, all of the yogurt, lemon, and the salt into a blender and whir to a smooth sauce. Add the rest of the cucumber and the seasonings, and stir.

Fresh Ricotta Cheese

Fresh ricotta cheese makes all the difference!   It's just delicious in lasagna or other dishes that call for ricotta, and it is super simple! Makes about 2 cups.

Ingredients:

- 4 cups whole milk
- 2 cups half and half
- 1 tablespoon lemon juice
- 1 3/4 tablespoons white wine vinegar
- 3/4 teaspoon salt

Directions:

Mix together the lemon and vinegar in a small dish and set aside. Bring milk, half and half, and salt to a simmer in a heavy sauce pan over low heat. Put lemon vinegar in, and simmer 1 minute if needed, but it should immediately turn into curds.

Put a double layer of cheesecloth over a strainer. Strain the water out of the cheese. Let sit until it reaches the desired firmness. For a more creamy ricotta, use immediately after straining.

Roasted Garlic Bread

This goes really well with spaghetti, meatballs, or minestrone soup. It will leave you wanting more... Serves 4 or more.

Ingredients:

1 fresh bread stick or French loaf, uncut
1/2 stick salted butter, softened
2 whole heads of garlic
extra virgin olive oil

Directions:

Make the roasted garlic ahead:

Preheat oven to 350 degrees (F). Leave the whole heads of garlic intact with paper. Using a sharp knife, cut through all of the tops (non-root side), just enough to expose the cloves. Place the heads of garlic on a piece of foil, and drizzle a little olive oil over the top of the exposed cloves. Bring up the corners of the foil together, and crinkle it closed to allow for roasting. Bake for 45 minutes to 1 hour. Check to see that it's done, it should be brown on top and soft inside. Let cool enough to handle, and remove the roasted garlic from the papers, and put in a small bowl. Mash the garlic all together, and add the softened butter, and mix. Set aside until ready to make the bread.

Cut the bread however you like it, in 1 inch slices or cut horizontally into lengths. Butter one side with the garlic butter and put all of the slices back together as a loaf. Put the bread into foil and bake until it's heated through, about 15-20 minutes. We like to leave some of the top of the bread exposed so the top gets a little crispy, while the center of the bread is soft. Serve while hot.

Desserts

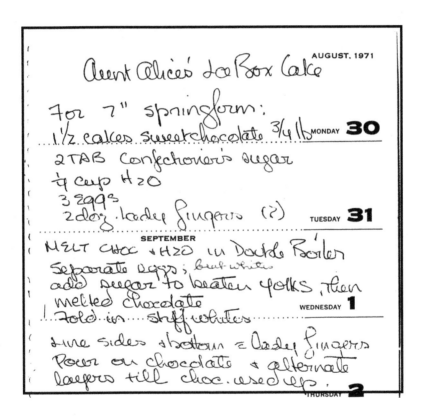

Aunt Alice's Ice Box Cake

AUGUST, 1971

For 7" springform:
1½ cakes sweet chocolate ¾ lb — MONDAY **30**
2 TAB Confectioner's sugar
¼ cup H2O
3 eggs
2 doz. Ladey fingers (?) — TUESDAY **31**

SEPTEMBER

MELT CHOC + H2O in Double Boiler
Separate eggs; beat whites
add sugar to beaten yolks, then
melted chocolate — WEDNESDAY **1**
Fold in stiff whites

Line sides + bottom ≡ Ladey fingers
Pour on chocolate + alternate
layers till choc. used up. — THURSDAY **2**

Fruit Turnovers

This can be made with any number of fruits; you can use apples, pears, nectarines, pineapple, plums, cherries, or berries of all types. Even a mix of fruits and berries works well. Best served hot with ice cream- Yum! Serves 4

Ingredients:

2 large apples, pears, or other fruit
1 puff pastry sheet -thawed
3 tablespoons brown sugar
1 tablespoon juice from lemon
1 tablespoon corn starch
1 egg white
1/2 teaspoon cinnamon
raw sugar to sprinkle on top

Directions:

Prepare a sheet pan: Place a silicone sheet liner on the pan. Alternately you can rub oil on foil to prevent sticking. Make egg wash by adding 1 tablespoon water to 1 egg white, and lightly beat with a fork. Set aside.

Roughly peel the pears or apples (or don't peel at all). Remove core, and cut into slices about 1/4 inch thick, then pieces. Stir in the lemon juice to keep from turning brown. Add the sugar, cornstarch, and cinnamon. Use filling immediately. The less amount of liquid in the fruit mixture, the easier it will be to prepare the turnovers and not have them leak while baking. If using berries, use white sugar instead of brown, and no need to add lemon.

Prepare the puff pastry: Dust the work surface with flour. Lay out the sheet flat, and use a rolling pin if needed to flatten it out. Do not work the pastry any more than is needed. Using a knife, divide the sheet into 4 or 9 squares, depending on the desired size.

Paint 2 edges of the pastry squares with egg wash- about 1/2 inch wide. Fill the middle with a heaping spoon full of fruit mixture, then fold over the pastry diagonally to form a triangle. Press the edges together to form a seal. Place the turnovers on the sheet pan. Cover with plastic wrap so they don't dry out while you are working. Paint the tops of the pastries with egg wash, and sprinkle with raw sugar.

Bake in an oven preheated to 400 degrees (F) for 20-25 minutes, until pastry is puffed up and golden brown.

Before baking, you can freeze them by lying out on a cookie sheet not touching. Once frozen, put a zip bag. You can pull out as many as you like, and thaw covered with plastic wrap. When ready, preheat the oven, and bake for 15-25 minutes. This makes an awesome dessert when having guests!

Aunt Alice's Ice Box Cake

John's Mom got this recipe from her Aunt Alice, and she passed it along to John, who is now passing it along to his family. Enjoy!

Ingredients:

8 ounces of semi-sweet chocolate squares
4 ounces of sweet chocolate squares
3 large eggs
2 tablespoons powdered sugar
1/4 cup hot water
2 dozen lady fingers
1 cup whipping cream
2 tablespoons powdered sugar
1 teaspoon vanilla extract

Directions:

In a 6 or 7 inch spring form pan, line the sides of the pan with lady fingers standing vertically right next to each other just like a picket fence. Line the bottom with lady fingers as well. Set pan aside. If you don't want your picket fence standing above the chocolate, simply cut the bottom bit off of each lady finger and use that piece to fill in more lady fingers in the bottom and middle layers.

Add chocolate and water to a double boiler, and heat until melted, stirring occasionally. Separate eggs, and beat the egg whites until stiff peaks form. In a separate bowl, beat the egg yolks, and add 2 tablespoons powdered sugar. Let the chocolate cool just a bit, then add a heaping tablespoon of hot chocolate to the egg yolks, and stir to temper the eggs. Add the egg mixture into the rest of the chocolate and stir. Once fully blended, using a spatula, gently fold in the egg whites into the chocolate mix a little at a time until incorporated.

Pour 1/2 chocolate mixture into the pan over the bottom layer of lady fingers. Add another layer of lady fingers and then the rest of the chocolate. Cover cake once completely cooled, and refrigerate for at least 6 hours.

When ready to serve, make whipped cream by beating cream until soft peaks form. Add powdered sugar and vanilla, and mix well. Serve cake with whipped cream, and garnish with chocolate shavings.

Fruit Crisp

This is a nice make-ahead dessert. You can make both the filling and the topping ahead, just don't assemble them until ready to bake.

You can use just about any fruit you have on hand- apples, pears, berries, or even pineapple. You can even mix fruits, such as peaches and blueberries, or pineapple and strawberries. It's awesome served hot out of the oven with a scoop of vanilla ice cream! Serves 4

Ingredients:

Filling:
- 2 large nectarines or peaches
- 1 cup blueberries
- 1 tablespoon lemon, squeezed onto fruit
- 2 tablespoons brown sugar
- 1 tablespoon corn starch

Topping:
- 2/3 cup brown sugar
- 1/2 cup flour
- 1/2 cup oats
- 1/4 cup nuts (optional)
- 1 teaspoon cinnamon
- 6 tablespoons butter

Directions:

If desired, rough-peel the nectarines, peaches, apples, or pears. Core, and cut into slices about 1/4 inch thick. Toss the fruit with the lemon, brown sugar, and corn starch, and let sit and macerate while you prepare the rest of the ingredients. If using only berries, lemon is not needed. Also, if the fruit was previously frozen and there is excess liquid, just add a little more corn starch.

Mix the topping dry ingredients in a separate bowl, then cut the butter into fairly small pieces (about 1/4 inch cubes), mix into dry ingredients.

Butter an 8x8 inch baking dish. Put filling in the dish, and sprinkle the topping mixture over the top. Bake for 30-40 minutes at 400 degrees (F), until the topping is golden brown.

Mud Pie

For many years, our kids have requested Mud Pie for their birthdays rather than a cake. So Mud Pie it is! We let them pick the second ice cream flavor. One kid likes cookie dough and the other likes cookies and cream. Just about anything chocolate goes well with the coffee ice cream. (They both like the classic coffee ice cream). This one shown is made with coffee and vanilla bean.

Make the pie ahead of time, then heat up the chocolate sauce, and make the whipped cream when ready to serve. The amount of ice cream you use depends on the size of spring form pan. This 6 inch pan uses 1 pint of each kind. A 9 inch pie pan or spring form will use 1 quart of each.

Ingredients:

1/2 package chocolate wafers, about 4-1/2 ounces.
4 tablespoons butter, melted
1 cup heavy cream
2 tablespoons powdered sugar
sliced toasted almonds

1 teaspoon vanilla extract
fudge sauce
coffee ice cream
other flavor ice cream

Directions:

Use a gallon zip bag to crush the chocolate wafers. If you cannot get chocolate wafers, you could use Oreo cookies without the middle instead. Mix the melted butter and chocolate crumbs. Pat the mixture into a very lightly buttered pie plate, or a spring-form pan. Meanwhile, soften the ice cream. Spread first the coffee ice cream on top of the crust, then the other flavor on top of that. Cover the ice cream with plastic wrap, and place in the freezer until ready to serve. This should sit in the freezer at least 4 hours prior to serving.

Just before serving, whip the cream together with the sugar and vanilla extract using a beater, until stiff peaks form. Refrigerate until ready to serve. Warm the fudge sauce and set aside.

Pull the pie out of the freezer. In order to get the pie to release, you may need to warm the outside of the pie plate or spring form pan by placing a hot damp towel around the outside. Use a knife dipped in hot water to slice. Place on serving plate. Drizzle hot fudge on each piece, and top with whipped cream. Sprinkle almonds on top and serve. Since the ice cream is cold, and the fudge sauce is hot, it wants to slide off of the ice cream. It's OK- it turns out to be a ooey-gooey yummy mess! Alternately, you can drizzle the hot chocolate sauce beside the ice cream on the plate.

Cheese Danishes

These lemony Danishes can be made as a delicious make-ahead dessert. If serving a crowd, you could cut the puff pastry into 9 squares instead of 4 and make them the same way, only smaller. The cooking time will vary a little.

Makes 4 pastries

Ingredients:

4 ounces cream cheese, at room temperature
1 extra-large egg yolk, at room temperature
1 teaspoon pure vanilla extract
1/4 cup sugar

1 teaspoon grated lemon zest, packed
1 sheet frozen puff pastry, thawed
1 egg white plus 1 tablespoon water

Optional glaze:

1/2 cup confectioners' sugar
2 teaspoons milk

Directions:

Cover the puff pastry while thawing. Preheat the oven to 400 degrees (F). Line a sheet pan with parchment paper or a silicone baking sheet.

Place the cream cheese and sugar in a bowl. Using a mixer, mix them together on low speed until smooth. With the mixer still on low, add the egg yolk, vanilla, and lemon zest, and mix until just combined well.

Unfold the sheet of puff pastry onto a lightly floured surface, and roll it slightly with a floured rolling pin until its square and flat. Don't work it more than you need to. Cut the sheet into 4 squares with a sharp knife. Move the puff pastry pieces to the sheet pan, removing any excess flour. Place a 1/4 of the cheese filling into the middle of each of the 4 squares. Brush the border of each pastry with egg wash and fold all 4 corners up just a little to be slightly touching the filling. Paint egg wash on the folded up corners.

Either bake right away, or refrigerate the filled pastries until ready to bake.

Bake the pastries for about 20 minutes, rotating the pan once during baking, until they are puffed and light brown. The filling will puff up a lot, but will reduce in size as they cool. Transfer to a wire rack, and let cool at least 10 minutes. If desired, drizzle glaze over them after they are completely cooled.

To make the glaze, place some of the confectioners' sugar into a small bowl. Stir in just a tiny bit of the milk at a time, until the mixture is a thick syrupy consistency. Pour mixture into a small plastic zip bag, and cut a small amount off one corner to make a piping bag. Stripe some glaze onto the pastries.

As an additional option instead of glaze, you could sprinkle a little raw sugar over the entire pastry after applying the egg wash. This gives them a little sweet crunch that really adds.

This can be a nice make-ahead dessert by refrigerating the pastries once assembled. Just paint them with egg wash, and then bake them just before dinner is served. Your guests are going to love them!

New York Cheesecake

Ingredients:

Cheesecake:
6 8-ounce packages cream cheese
  (Philadelphia brand is preferred)
1 3/4 cups granulated sugar
3 tablespoons all-purpose flour
2 teaspoons grated lemon zest
1 teaspoon vanilla
5 jumbo eggs
2 jumbo egg yolks
1/2 cup heavy cream

Crust:
15 graham crackers
8 tablespoons butter, melted

Directions:

Be sure the oven rack is in the middle of the oven. Preheat oven to 350 degrees (F). Have all ingredients at room temperature. Lightly butter a 9 inch spring form pan. Note: 1/2 of a recipe will make a 6-inch spring form pan. The cooking time will be similar.

Place the graham crackers in a plastic zip bag, and crush them to medium fine. Pour into a mixing bowl, and mix in the melted butter. Press the crumbs into the bottom of the spring form pan.

Using a hand mixer beat the cream cheese in a large bowl until creamy. Do not over-beat. Gradually add the sugar and flour; mix until smooth and creamy, scraping the beaters and sides of bowl, about 1 to 2 minutes. Mix in the lemon zest and vanilla. Mix in the eggs and yolks one at a time, just until each is incorporated, scraping the bowl and the beaters often. On low speed, mix in the cream.

Scrape the batter onto the crust, and smooth the top. Bake for 50 minutes, and then check to see if it's done by opening the oven door, and gently wiggling the pan. It's done if only the center is still really wet and soft. Cook 5-10 minutes longer if needed. Once it's mostly cooked, turn the oven off and open the oven door part way. Let the cake cool in oven without moving it, until completely cool, a couple of hours. Once 100% room temperature, cover and refrigerate for a few hours before serving.

Almond Flour Blueberry Muffins

Makes 6 Muffins

Ingredients:

- 1 5/8 cups almond flour
- 3/4 teaspoon baking soda
- 1/8 teaspoon kosher salt
- 2 large eggs, room temperature
- 1 mashed ripe banana (or can use 1/2 cup apple sauce)
- 1 tablespoons honey
- 1 1/3 tablespoons melted coconut oil
- 1/8 teaspoon rice vinegar
- 1 teaspoon vanilla extract
- 1 tsp orange zest or 1/2 teaspoon orange extract
- 1 cup blueberries

Directions:

Preheat oven to 350 degrees (F). Line 6 cups in a standard muffin pan with paper liners.

In a large bowl, mix the almond flour, baking soda, and salt. In a separate small bowl, whisk the eggs, banana, honey, oil, vinegar, extract, and zest. Add the wet ingredients to the dry ingredients, and stir until blended. Fold in the blueberries.

Divide batter evenly among prepared cups. Bake in preheated oven for 18-22 minutes, until the centers are set and the edges are golden brown. Move the pan to a cooling rack, and let muffins cool in the pan 30 minutes. Remove muffins from pan, and serve while warm.

Pumpkin Bars

Serves 4-6

Ingredients:

1/2 cup roasted pumpkin or squash
1/2 cup sugar or substitute
2 large eggs
1 cup blanched almond flour
1/4 teaspoon kosher salt
1/2 teaspoon baking soda
1 teaspoon ground cinnamon
1/8 teaspoon ground nutmeg
1/8 teaspoon cloves
3/4 cup chopped nuts if desired

Cream Cheese Frosting:

4 ounces cream cheese, room temperature
1 tablespoon butter, room temperature
1/3 cup sugar or substitute
1 teaspoon vanilla extract
1-2 tablespoons half and half, as needed

Directions:

For sugar substitute, Erythritol or Xylitol (sugar alcohols) work well for this recipe. If using Erythritol granules, use a spice grinder to make into powder.

Using a mixer, combine pumpkin, sugar or substitute, and eggs, and beat with mixer until well blended. In a separate large bowl, combine dry ingredients and mix well. Add dry ingredients into the wet ingredients, and mix a full minute until well combined. Add a bit of water if needed. If you use extra-large eggs, water may not be needed to obtain a cake batter consistency. Stir in nuts if desired

Pour batter into a greased 8 x 8 inch baking pan. Bake at 350 degrees (F) for 30-35 minutes, until golden brown. A toothpick stuck in the middle should come out clean if it's cooked through. Cool completely.

Note: If making muffins instead of bars, cook about 25-30 minutes. As usual, when baking with almond flour instead of wheat flour, baked goods can be a bit crumbly. Bars tend to hold together better than muffins in this application.

Frosting: Use a mixer to combine cream cheese, butter, sugar, and vanilla. Add half and half a little at a time if needed to get a creamy consistency.

Cinnamon Puff Pastry Straws

These make a great small dessert for a Mexican meal. Beware- you're going to need plates and napkins, they are super flaky and delicious!

Serves 4

Ingredients:

puff pastry- 1 sheet, thawed
1/2 cup sugar
3 teaspoons ground cinnamon
1-2 tablespoons butter, melted
white from 1 egg

Directions:

Preheat oven to 375 degrees (F). Line a baking sheet with a silicone sheet or parchment paper.

Keep puff pastry refrigerated until ready to use. Lay the pastry sheet out on a lightly floured surface. Using a rolling pin, gently roll it to just flatten it, but don't work it more than necessary. It will be square; cut it in half with a knife horizontally.

Mix the sugar and cinnamon together in a small dish or jar with sprinkle-lid. Paint butter on the left 1/2 of one rectangle. Sprinkle a bunch of cinnamon/sugar on the butter until it is all covered but the cinnamon-sugar is moistened. Fold the right side of the pastry over onto the left side like a book. Roll out to press the pastry horizontally a little. Paint with butter again on half the rectangle, and sprinkle with cinnamon sugar again, and then fold like a book again. Roll a little to seal it. Repeat with second half of puff pastry.

Use a sharp knife and cut into 1/4 to 3/8 inch wide strips. If there are folded edges, simply cut them off and discard. Take each strip and twist it, and lay it on the baking sheet and with ends separated. This will make them all crazy and fun looking once they cook.

Lightly beat the egg white and add 1 tablespoon of water. Brush the tops of each straw with the egg wash and sprinkle cinnamon sugar over the top. Bake the straws for 12-18 minutes, until they are golden brown, puffed up, and crispy. Use a spatula to move to a cooling rack. Let cool a few minutes before serving.

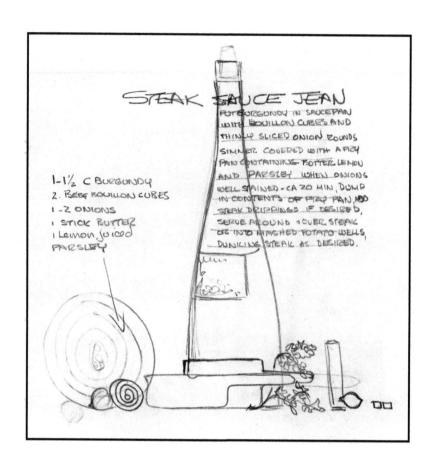

STEAK SAUCE JEAN

PUT BURGUNDY IN SAUCEPAN WITH BOUILLON CUBES AND THINLY SLICED ONION ROUNDS SIMMER COVERED WITH A FRY PAN CONTAINING BUTTER LEMON AND PARSLEY WHEN ONIONS WELL STAINED ~ CA 20 MIN, DUMP IN CONTENTS OF FRY PAN ADD STEAK DRIPPINGS IF DESIRED, SERVE AROUND + OVER STEAK OR INTO MASHED POTATO WELLS, DUNKING STEAK AS DESIRED.

1-1½ C BURGUNDY
2. BEEF BOUILLON CUBES
1-2 ONIONS
1 STICK BUTTER
1 Lemon juiced
PARSLEY

Sauces and Seasonings

Homemade Stone Ground Mustard

Makes about 1 cup

Ingredients:

3 tablespoons yellow mustard seeds
3 tablespoons brown mustard seeds
3 tablespoons white wine
1/3 cup white wine vinegar
1/4 teaspoon salt

Directions:

Mix ingredients together, and let sit covered on at room temperature for 3 days for spicy mustard. If non-spicy is desired, put mustard seeds in liquids into refrigerator immediately. Shake or stir occasionally.

If you desire 100 percent stone-ground, then just use whole mustard seeds. If you desire partially creamy/ partially stone-ground, then using a spice grinder, grind 1/2 of each type of seeds and mix the powder with the remaining seeds.

After a few days, the seeds will absorb the liquids. If after a few days it's too liquidy, simply add a couple of tablespoons more seeds. It should tighten up in a day. If it seems too dry, you can add a teaspoon or two of water.

Mustard lasts for months in the fridge. Couldn't be simpler!!

BBQ Sauce

John has been making this same BBQ sauce for many, many years for BBQ ribs or chicken cooked on the grill. Delicious! Makes about 2 cups.

Ingredients:

3/4 cup ketchup
3/4 cup dark brown sugar
1/4 cup Worcestershire sauce
1/4 cup low sodium soy sauce
1/4 cup red wine vinegar

1/2 teaspoon garlic powder
1/2 teaspoon onion powder
1/2 teaspoon freshly ground pepper
2 tablespoons yellow mustard

Directions:

Mix well all ingredients. It keeps in the fridge for a number of months.

Teresa's Low-Carb Version

Use the same recipe as above, except use reduced-sugar ketchup, and use Xylitol (sugar alcohol) or other sugar substitute instead of brown sugar. A bit of cayenne pepper added is good as well!

Tartar Sauce

This tartar sauce goes really great with white fish such as cod or halibut, as well as salmon.

Makes 1 to 1 1/2 cups

Ingredients:

3/4 cup mayonnaise (Best Foods or Hellmann's)
1/4 cup very finely diced or grated sweet onion
1/4 cup very finely diced or grated dill pickle
3 tablespoons fresh lemon juice, or to taste
1 teaspoon fresh or dried dill weed

Directions:

Mix all of the ingredients together, and put into a serving dish. Refrigerate at least 1-2 hours before serving.

Homemade Cocktail Sauce

We cannot believe how easy and delicious this is. We never buy pre-made cocktail sauce anymore! Using a good quality ketchup, such as Portland Brand, makes all the difference. Serve this with cooked shrimp and crab.

Ingredients:

- 3-4 tablespoons Prepared Fresh Horseradish (see recipe)
- 1 cup ketchup
- 2 tablespoons juice from lemon
- 1/2 teaspoon Worcestershire sauce
- 1/4 teaspoon salt
- 1/4 teaspoon freshly ground pepper

Directions:

Mix all ingredients together, and refrigerate for 2 hours before serving.

Prepared Fresh Horseradish

Ingredients:

    1 horseradish root, about 1 1/2 inches in diameter x 6 inches long
    4 tablespoons cold water
    4 tablespoons white wine vinegar

Directions:

Cut the ends from the horseradish root, and peel the outside skin off. Chop it into small pieces. Add the water and root pieces to a food processor or blender, and whir until finely grated. Use a spatula to get all of the horseradish processed. You could also grate the root using a grater, and stir water into it.

When processing or grating, the horseradish is very pungent and spicy (and delicious!) Take care to not breath in the fumes.

If you like spicy horseradish, wait about 3 minutes after processing to add the vinegar, and stir it in well. Adding vinegar will stop it from getting hotter. If you want the horseradish to be mild, just add it immediately after processing.

Put the amount you might use in 2-3 weeks into a small glass jar, and refrigerate. You can freeze the rest in portion sizes for future use!

If you want to serve Creamy Horseradish Sauce (goes awesome with beef!), just add some of this Prepared Fresh Horseradish to sour cream to your desired level of spice!

Homemade Enchilada Sauce

Ancho chilis (dried poblanos) can be spicy hot. Some are and some are not. If you really don't want spicy enchilada sauce, you should taste them first and determine if there is a spicy one among them. You could sub one or both whole ancho chilis for 1 tablespoon of ancho chili powder each.

Ingredients:

2 tablespoons extra virgin olive oil

3 cloves garlic, minced

1 cup chopped yellow onion

1 teaspoon dried oregano

5 teaspoons ancho chili powder

1/4 teaspoon freshly ground pepper

1/2 teaspoon salt

1 1/2 teaspoon ground cumin

2 teaspoons dried or 2 tablespoons fresh parsley

1 15-ounce can diced tomatoes, with juice

2 whole dried ancho chilis

2 cups pepper water (see instructions)

1/4 chopped jalapeño, seeds removed

2-3 tablespoons fresh cilantro

Directions:

Bring 3 cups of water to a boil. Remove the stems, seeds, and veins from the ancho chilis. Chop into large chunks and add to a blender. Add 2 cups of the water to blender, and whir until smooth. Be sure to hold the lid tight so you don't get burned. Let it sit and steep while you chop and sauté veggies. If making multiple batches, don't whir more than 2 cups at a time in the blender, or it could become a big, boiling mess!

Heat the olive oil in a large saucepan over medium heat. Add the garlic, onion, and jalapeño, and sauté until soft. Then add oregano, chili powder, black pepper, salt, cumin, parsley, and stir. Add cilantro, tomatoes, chili water, plus 1 more cup of boiling water.

Bring to the boil, reduce heat to low, and simmer for 20 to 25 minutes uncovered. Cover the pot if it looks like it's getting too thick. Take off the heat and cool. Blend smooth using a blender or stick blender. Let simmer to thicken if needed after blending.

Use with enchiladas, tamales, or chili rellenos. You can also freeze this sauce in portion sizes.

Arrabiata Sauce

This is a great marinara sauce to be used on Pasta or Meatballs. Arrabiata in Italian means *angry*- it's intended to be a bit spicy! (not to mention delicious...!)

Ingredients:

extra virgin olive oil for sautéing
1 28-ounce can tomatoes
1/2 6-ounce can tomato paste
1/4 cup red wine
3/4-1 teaspoon red pepper flakes
1 tablespoon chopped fresh basil

3 tablespoons fresh oregano, chopped
1 tablespoon fresh marjoram, chopped
3 tablespoon chopped fresh parsley
1/8 teaspoon ground black pepper
1/3-1/2 cup chopped yellow onion
3 cloves garlic
salt to taste

Directions:

Sauté onions and garlic in olive oil for 5 minutes (just to soften), then add the rest of the ingredients, and simmer for 15-20 minutes. Use stick blender to make sauce as smooth as you like.

If using meat in the sauce, create the marinara sauce, whir it smooth, then add the meat and let simmer 2-3 hours. This makes *Gravy* according to some Italian cooking experts. You may need to add some water as it cooks.

If cooking a long time, I add half of the fresh herbs up front, and then add the rest when the meat sauce is almost done. That helps to incorporate the flavors of the herbs, while keeping the bright herb flavor.

Marinara Sauce

Ingredients:

1 28-ounce cans crushed tomatoes
  -or- 2 pounds ripe plum tomatoes, skinned and seeded
1 6-ounce can tomato paste
1/4 cup extra-virgin olive oil
3/4 medium yellow onion or 1/2 large, chopped
1 garlic clove, finely chopped
1 celery rib, chopped
1/2 small carrot, chopped
1/2 teaspoon freshly ground black pepper
salt to taste
2 dried bay leaves
12 leaves fresh basil, chopped
1 teaspoon dried oregano

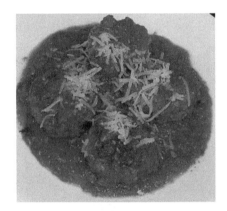

Directions:

In a large pot, heat the oil to medium. Add the onions, and sauté until the onions soften, about 15 minutes. Throw in the garlic and sauté for 3-4 minutes more. Add the celery, carrots, and 1/2 teaspoon ground pepper. Sauté until all the vegetables are soft, about 10 minutes. Add the tomatoes to the pot, rinse out the empty tomato can with water, and add that water to the pot (about 1/2 cup). Add bay leaves, basil, and oregano. Simmer about 2 hours uncovered over low heat. Taste for seasonings, adding more salt and pepper as needed.

Use a stick blender to blend smooth, or can use a blender working in batches. If the sauce is too thin, put back on the stove and simmer uncovered a little more. If the sauce seems too thick, you can add a little water and bring back to a boil.

You can also make multiple batches, and freeze in portion sizes for future use.

Mexi Mix Seasoning

John makes this seasoning mix ahead in large quantities since it's used in a variety of our Mexican dishes. Chili powders you typically find in the grocery store are a combination of chili powder, garlic, cumin, salt, etc. We like to make our own mix so we can limit the quantity of salt, and this tastes so much brighter.

When we make meat for tacos or other Mexican dishes, we typically use about 2 1/2 to 3 tablespoons of this mix for a pound of meat. But how much may be different for each dish and according to your taste. Since we don't add salt to this seasoning, some salt may be need to be added to the dish you are using it in.

Ingredients:

3 parts ancho chili powder
1 1/2 part cumin
1 part ground coriander
1/2 part garlic powder
1/2 part onion powder

Directions:

Mix in a large bowl, and pour into jars, and then label.

Greek Seasoning Mix

We like to have this Greek seasoning on hand to help with delicious quick meals. Just sprinkle on strips of lamb and fry to make it taste like gyro meat. You could also put a little olive oil on a pita and sprinkle on a little of this seasoning, then fry the pita to get it warmed and just a little brown. Add the meat and some chopped veggies and it makes the best gyro sandwich ever!

Ingredients:

2-1/2 teaspoons dried oregano
1 tablespoon garlic powder
1 tablespoon freshly ground pepper
1 tablespoon dried parsley
1-1/2 tablespoons onion powder
3/4 tablespoon cinnamon
1/2 tablespoon nutmeg
1 tablespoon dried thyme
1 teaspoon dried mint (optional)

Directions:

Mix in a bowl. Pour into a spice-size jar, and then label.

Breakfast

Granola Cereal

Ingredients:

1/3 cup maple syrup (or raw honey)
1/3 cup brown sugar
1/2 cup extra virgin olive oil
1/4 teaspoon salt
5 teaspoons vanilla extract
2 cups chopped nuts
5 cups regular old fashioned oats

Directions:

Mix the first 5 ingredients in a large bowl, and then add the oats and nuts. Line cookie sheet with parchment paper, and press mixture firmly into the bottom of pan.

Bake at 325 degrees (F) for 15 minutes, and then turn mixture over using a spatula. Be sure to press it down firmly into the pan. Cook 13-15 more minutes, until starting to turn toasty brown. Do not overcook. It can go from light brown to over-cooked very quickly.

Let cool 1 hour.

Break into chunks. Add dried fruit or toasted coconut flakes if desired after baking.

Keeps up to several weeks in a glass jar.

Granola Bars

Makes a 9 x 12 inch pan

Ingredients:

1 1/2 cups rolled oats
1 1/2 cups chopped nuts of your choice
1 cup shredded unsweetened coconut
1 cup seeds, toasted- pumpkin or sunflower
2/3 cup coconut oil, melted
3/4 cup raw honey
2 tablespoons vanilla extract
1/4 teaspoon sea salt
1 cup dried fruit
3 teaspoons cinnamon

Directions:

Preheat oven. Line an 11 x 7-inch baking pan with parchment paper so the sides of paper overhang. Use coconut oil to very lightly coat any uncovered sides of pan.

Toast oats by spreading on a cookie sheet or large baking pan. Bake at 350 degrees (F) for 10-15 minutes until lightly browned. This gives the oats a nutty flavor and helps the mixture stick together better.

Mix toasted oats, nuts, seeds, and shredded coconut into large bowl. In a small saucepan over low heat, mix wet ingredients, as well as salt and cinnamon until fully incorporated. Add wet ingredients to the dry ingredients, and stir until mixed well. Add dried fruit at the end. Spread mixture into pan and tamp it down.

Bake for 15 minutes at 350 degrees (F) degrees, and then turn the oven down to 325 degrees (F) degrees and bake for another 10 minutes, until golden brown.

Remove pan from oven, and cool it completely. Invert pan onto a cutting board, and the block of bars should pop out of the pan. Cut into bars. Store in refrigerator, or freeze for future use.

Breakfast Smoothies

Serves 4

Ingredients:

  2 cups Greek yogurt
  2 bananas, thawed (see below)
  1 1/2 cups other fruit (see below)
  almond milk

Directions:

Use blender to puree all the fruit and yogurt. If too thick, you can use a splash of almond milk. Once it's the desired consistency, add ice cubes (about 8 or 10), and blend until smooth and cold.

We buy bananas by the bunch, and with kids no longer in the house eating everything in sight, we often have bananas left over. These freeze perfectly for smoothies! Just peel them, put them in a large zip bag, and throw them in the freezer. You can grab 1 or 2 frozen bananas for smoothies and defrost them in the microwave, or set them in a dish on the counter. They are not good for just eating since they get mushy once you freeze them. We also use these frozen bananas in cooking, such as Almond Flour Blueberry Muffins. They act as a delicious natural sweetener.

As for the other fruit, we tend to buy what's in season locally. Nectarines, grapes, blueberries, pineapple, tangerines, mangos, cherries. They all make great smoothies! We freeze some of the other fruits to use in smoothies throughout the year. If you're fruit is not super sweet, not to worry, your ripe bananas will sweeten your smoothie for you.

Other options for breakfast smoothies include adding protein powder or flax seed. A delicious way to start your day!

Potato Breakfast Casserole

Serves 4

Ingredients:

3 medium potatoes, fully baked and cooled
1/2 to 3/4 pound ham, diced to about 1/2 inch cubes
2 medium tomatoes, diced
3-4 green onions, chopped
1 1/2 cups grated cheddar cheese
1/2 cup sour cream
1/4 teaspoon paprika
olive oil

Directions:

Bake potatoes the day ahead to make breakfast an easy meal. Cook, cool, then peel (or don't), and cut them into 1/2 inch cubes. Refrigerate until time to use.

Preheat oven to 350 degrees (F). Put some olive oil in a fry pan, and toss in potatoes, ham, and paprika. Heat though, stirring occasionally. Remove from heat, and stir in diced tomatoes. Put mixture in a baking dish. Spread cheddar cheese over the top, and bake for 10-15 minutes until the cheese is melted thoroughly. Pull out of the oven, and serve with sour cream and green onions on top.

There are a number of variations that can be done with this dish. Try using chorizo or other pre-cooked sausage instead of ham. You could also add a little cayenne to spice it up! Diced tomatoes can be added after baking instead of before baking as well.

This makes a great dish for a breakfast with family or friends.

Latkes (Potato Pancakes)

These can be made as a side dish, or as a breakfast item. We like them in both cases!

Ingredients:

2 medium potatoes, grated
1/2 large onion, grated
1/4 cup flour
1 egg
1/2 teaspoon salt
pinch of freshly ground pepper
oil for frying- avocado or olive oil
cheesecloth for draining potatoes and onions

Directions:

Grate the potatoes and onions. Line a bowl with a piece of cheesecloth, and pour the grated potatoes and onions into the cheesecloth. Twist the cloth closed, and wring until the excess liquids are gone. Transfer to a clean, dry bowl, and mix in the rest of the ingredients.

You could also grate the potatoes, put them into salted water to keep them from turning brown, then drain them and squeeze the excess liquid out. This would be the method if you are chopping the onions instead of grating them. You could use green, red, or yellow onions in these- whatever you have on hand.

Heat a frying pan to medium, and add oil. When hot, add large spoonsful to the pan until the patties are 1/4 to 1/2 inch thick. Cook on both sides until brown, making sure they are cooked through. Serve while hot.

Serve with applesauce, sour cream, and diced green onions, or sour cream and caviar.

Huevos Rancheros

Serves 4

Ingredients:

4 corn tortillas
8 eggs
1 cup enchilada sauce
-or- Salsa Ranchera (Herdez brand)
1/2 cup grated cheddar cheese

1/2 cup sour cream
2 ripe avocados, sliced
hash brown potatoes
black beans (optional)

Directions:

You can use Enchilada Sauce (see recipe), or use canned Salsa Ranchera.

Coat corn tortillas with oil, and bake on cookie sheet until golden brown and crispy, turning once towards the end. Bake about 15 mins at 350 degrees (F). This can be done ahead of time.

Cook hash browns. You can use fresh or frozen. Heat up ranchera sauce.

Once hash browns are browned, cook eggs as desired. I like sunny side up, others preferred scrambled, etc.

Assemble the Huevos Rancheros: Hash browns first, 1 crispy tortilla, beans if using, then 2 cooked eggs, and about 3 tablespoons enchilada sauce. Sprinkle with cheddar cheese over the hot sauce, and serve with sour cream and avocado slices.

Bagels with Lox and Cream Cheese

This is a nice way to feed a crowd for brunch. It's easy to make a platter, and then let people help themselves. The bagels can be served toasted or not toasted as desired.

Sample Ingredients:

plain or sesame bagels, 1 per person- cut in half horizontally

cream cheese

lox (cold-smoked salmon), about 1-2 ounces per person

thin sliced sweet or red onion

English cucumber, sliced thin

sliced tomatoes

capers

olives

steamed chilled asparagus

chilled roasted red peppers

fresh green pepper, sliced lemon slices

About Freezing and Canning

We prefer to eat foods that are all natural, and we like to not eat the chemicals that you often find in so many prepared foods. We still buy a few prepared items, but that list is getting shorter each year.

When we buy beef, we typically buy 1/2 of an organic, grass-fed cow. This gives us good tasting, healthy meat, and doing it this way is more economical than buying the same meat in a grocery store. The challenge of using every piece of meat you get with 1/2 of a cow is fun- we dream up what to have for dinner tonight based on what's in the freezer.

We also look for whole chickens on sale and buy a lot of them when they are, and then we spend the time and effort to cut them up, and package them in portion sizes. We do the same thing with pork, lamb, and prawns.

We end up with our own homemade beef and chicken broth in the freezer that really adds to the flavors in many of our soups and other dishes.

Some of the dishes in this book can be a lot of work, such as Dolmathes or Spring Rolls, but we typically save those for a day when we have the time and are in the mood to cook. We make some for tonight and the rest for the freezer. It's pretty amazing how well some of these things freeze and reheat. Having some pre-made dishes in the freezer is really helpful for busy days.

We tend to freeze more than can. Canning some veggies like tomatoes is much more involved than freezing them, but canning Pickled Jalapeños or our own Grape Leaves is so simple and inexpensive, not to mention delicious! We like to have roasted peppers like poblanos, pimentos, and red bell peppers, on hand for various dishes, such as Chili Rellenos, Pimento Cheese Spread, Italian Beef Sandwiches, and others. When we pick them, we roast and seed them, and package them in small packages, and freeze them to use throughout the year. See the Chili Rellenos or Chicken Tortilla Soup recipes to see how to roast them.

Index

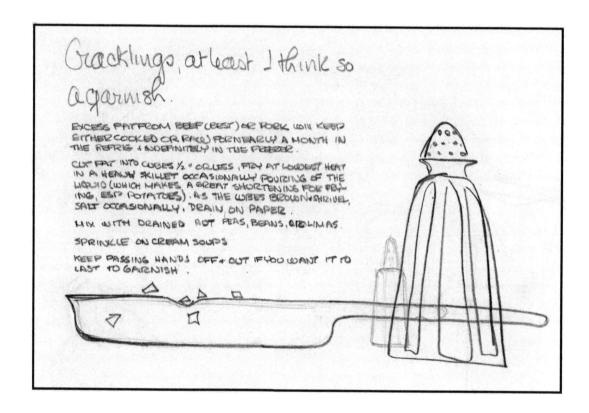

Cracklings, at least I think so
a garnish.

EXCESS FAT FROM BEEF (BEST) OR PORK WILL KEEP
EITHER COOKED OR RAW) FOR NEARLY A MONTH IN
THE REFRIG & INDEFINITELY IN THE FREEZER.

CUT FAT INTO CUBES ½" OR LESS, FRY AT LOWEST HEAT
IN A HEAVY SKILLET OCCASIONALLY POURING OF THE
LIQUID (WHICH MAKES A GREAT SHORTENING FOR FRY-
ING, ESP POTATOES). AS THE CUBES BROWN & SHRIVEL,
SALT OCCASIONALLY, DRAIN ON PAPER.

MIX WITH DRAINED HOT PEAS, BEANS, OR LIMAS.

SPRINKLE ON CREAM SOUPS

KEEP PASSING HANDS OFF & OUT IF YOU WANT IT TO
LAST TO GARNISH.

235

About the Authors

John and Teresa Polk have been married for 36 years. They live in the Seattle area for most of the year, and in Tucson part of the year. They both retired in 2011 from the aerospace industry, and began working on projects long postponed, this book being one. They enjoy exploring the local area and around the U.S., as well as traveling internationally.

John and Teresa have 2 sons and a daughter-in-law, with the oldest son and his wife living in Hawaii. They cherish the times to visit with them, whether in Seattle, Tucson or Hawaii!

Cooking and eating good food has always been part of our family. Experiencing different cuisines around the world and in the U.S. has inspired us to continue to expand our knowledge of the food, the people, and the cultures.

facebook.com/teresa polk

CPSIA information can be obtained
at www.ICGtesting.com
Printed in the USA
BVOW05s0620201117
500892BV00023B/1082/P

9 780692 978603